*The*
# CHRISTOLOGY OF
## *ROSEMARY RADFORD*
# RUETHER

## *A Critical Introduction*

## Mary Hembrow Snyder

# TWENTY-THIRD PUBLICATIONS
**Mystic, Connecticut**

The **cover photo** of Rosemary Radford Ruether is provided
through the courtesy of Garrett-Evangelical Theological Seminary.

Twenty-Third Publications
185 Willow Street
P.O. Box 180
Mystic CT 06355
(203) 536-2611

ISBN 0-89622-358-2
Library of Congress Catalog Number 87-51564

In memory of
my mother
Dorothy Hembrow Cizanckas Snyder
(1919-1983)

and

my maternal grandmother
Madeline Bracklo Hembrow Kessler
(1900-1983)

two women who loved me well
and
taught me to live passionately

# Preface

> And the only kind of pain that is
> intolerable is pain that is
> wasteful, pain from which we
> do not learn.
>
> *Audre Lorde*

> ...how you understand suffering
> determines how you understand
> God and Jesus.
>
> *Rosemary Radford Ruether*

Pain, one of my greatest teachers during the past several years, has taught me, more than anything else, that the personal is political. The recognition of this truth by women is feminism's particular contribution to political theory, and therefore to political theology. This volume marks the end of one stage of my political and theological education, and can only be fully understood in the context of this education.

My only sibling, a brother, died of a heart attack in November 1980 at 43 years of age. On December 2, 1980, a few weeks after my brother's death, four missionary women from the United States were murdered in El Salvador. This tragedy politicized me as nothing ever had before. I began to realize that everything is linked: U.S. hegemony and Latin American oppression, ideological blindness and "keeping the world safe for democracy," capitalism and militarism, rampant social sin and a privatized faith, commitment to the poor and the oppressed, and martyrdom.

The violent deaths of the missionary women led me to my first participation in a political demonstration. I marched on the Pentagon the following May with thousands of others protesting U.S. President Ronald Reagan's policy in El Salvador. Indirectly, the deaths of those four women made me more certain that I had to simplify my lifestyle and become more concretely involved in justice issues and education.

In June 1981, I left the religious community I had been with since 1966; faced with the task of reconstructing my life, I moved to Toronto and began a doctoral program in theology.

During this time my mother was confined to a hospital with an inoperable brain tumor that was slowly devouring her life. Since I had no other immediate family (my father had died of cancer when I was 13 years old), my mother needed me. At least one weekend a month I would go to Buffalo, N.Y., to be with her, but the frequency of those trips away from my studies increased as her condition worsened. As I struggled to participate in her dying, my energy waned and I experienced the gulf that exists between theological education and the reality of human suffering. As a result, I became deeply committed to trying to bridge that gap.

My mother died, and a month later I left for Peru where I was to do some research on feminism in a Latin American context. During my time there I made valuable contacts with some Limanean feminists and U.S. missionary women who were also dedicated feminists. Through them I was exposed to a Third World feminist view of the church and society. The trip left an indelible mark on my theological/political perspective for several reasons. First, the suffering and injustice I witnessed confirmed much of the liberation theology I had been studying in terms of the plight of the poor and the oppressed in the Third World. Second, the trip opened my eyes to the multi-layered suffering of poor, Third World women afflicted not only by sexism, but racism and classism as well. Their condition concretized for me the insights of feminist theologians that there is a profound connection between sexism, racism, classism, and imperialism. Third, the trip helped me to perceive my mother's difficult life and death in larger terms; they were related to the fact that she was a working-class woman. Thus, I began to realize that her suffering was part of the much larger reality of suffering experienced by women all over the world. And while the layers and degrees of that suffering certainly differed according to racial and class status, what remained common was the global reality of women's experience of suffering.

I left Peru with a clearer understanding that "the personal is political." At the same time, the trip deepened my already ripening conviction that both my life and the theology I was attempting to do had no business being anywhere except on the side of the poor and oppressed.

On November 22, 1983, seven months after my mother's death, my maternal grandmother also died. I was very close to her and this second profound loss in so short a time was very difficult. Yet, it underlined my growing awareness of the link between my personal sorrows and the social injustice I perceived was taking place in Peru.

As I struggled with my experiences of pain and loss, I spent a good deal of time reflecting on the meaning of suffering. My theological studies and the sharing of stories with feminist and non-feminist women friends coalesced to help me see further that my experiences of suffering were very much linked to the corresponding social reality of suffering. They were not private burdens given to me by a masochistic God who willed them in my best interest. Thus, I needed to touch a deeper reality of God in all of this, for I refused to accept the easy answers religion so often put forth about such matters. I was coming to understand more clearly how closely related the personal is with the political, and theories that God sent suffering as trials to test, punish or purify us were repugnant to me. I also felt such theories violated the dignity of those who were powerless in their suffering.

Consequently, my experiences on both personal and political levels poignantly began to intersect over the meaning of suffering and the role God played. I had arrived at a global understanding of suffering and was in need of a new understanding of God and of Jesus. I found Dorothee Soelle's ideas of God and suffering very helpful in this regard, but Rosemary Radford Ruether's clearer efforts to identify suffering on a socio-political level as sexism, racism, classism, and imperialism encouraged me to pursue her understanding of God through her understanding of Jesus.

She wrote in a letter to me:

> ...if one rejects a masochistic, passive, fatalistic view of suffering for one that seeks dynamically to overcome the causes of suffering, then one will also reject a doctrine of crucifixion that reenforces masochistic, passive, fatalistic suffering in favor of discovering a Christ who suffers because he is in opposition to structures of injustice.[1]

These words encouraged me to pursue her christological vision. I would pursue an understanding of suffering that comprehends the truth of God as one who, "revealed in Jesus, has identified with the victims of history and has abandoned the thrones of the mighty,"[2] and that relates personal suffering with social suffering.

Ruether's christological position resonates deeply with my own experience. It arises from a critique of ahistorical and apolitical understandings of Jesus. Against anti-Judaic and exclusivist christologies that have contributed so keenly to the suffering of the Jews, it seeks to affirm the religious integrity of Judaism and other religious traditions. Against christological positions that denigrate women, it heralds women's dignity and full personhood with men and is rooted in the message and praxis of Jesus who sided first with the poor and oppressed. In response to the destructive humanocentrism[3] that has characterized Western civilization, it values the wholeness and goodness of creation.

As a Christian feminist committed to education for justice, whose roots are working-class and who still believes one's life can make a difference, I have found that Ruether's christological critique and alternative vision have given me not only enthusiasm and inspiration, but also hope. This hope means that Jesus can be a model for salvation, but only to the extent that we do not abandon one another *in this world*, in the struggle to overcome the causes of suffering and injustice.

# Acknowledgments

This book is the fruit of several years of study and struggle. Many people have made its completion possible.

Some of those people were men like Matthew Lamb, Daniel Maguire, and Dennis Doherty who were my teachers when I began graduate studies in theology at Marquette University ten years ago. To this day I am grateful for what they taught me at that period in my life, and for the larger vision of reality they challenged me to explore.

Another group of people who helped to make this book possible was my family and friends in Buffalo, New York, who never ceased to support me during the process of writing this manuscript. I thank my aunts and uncles, Fran and Gene Cassidy, Kate and Ed Mucha, Miriam Hembrow Morris and Herbert Morris (Coos Bay, Oregon), as well as my dear friends, Anne Marie Fitzsimmons, RSM, Renee and Steve Kos, Joanne Miranda Goodspeed, Virginia and Sandy Rizzo, Dolores McKenzie and Denise McKenzie, Mary Caruana, and Marian Grimes. I also thank the Sisters of Mercy, Diocese of Buffalo, for all they have given me over the years.

To my professors at the University of St. Michael's College, Toronto, I owe a great debt of gratitude. Among them I thank Mary Rose D'Angelo, Roger Haight, S.J., and Lee Cormie. Most especially, however, I thank Ellen Leonard, who so patiently and generously "mid-wifed" this manuscript in its dissertation stages. Each of these women and men helped me to rethink critically my worldview and supported my efforts to articulate Ruether's christological perspective.

Carter Heyward once wrote, "If I love you I have to make you conscious of the things you don't see." During my four years in Toronto, my Canadian women-friends did this for me. Such love deeply influenced the writing of this book. Thus, I am profoundly grateful to the following women: Mary Thompson Boyd, Marilyn Legge, Shelly Finson, Marsha Sfeir, Laurie Bell, Nicki Monahan, Janet Silman, and Diane Marshall. My vision is more whole today because of the consciousness they so lovingly raised in me.

I spent six weeks in Peru before I began writing the initial material for this book. That time was an intense learning experience and two women, in particular, left an indelible mark on my consciousness. They are Maryknoll Sisters Rose Dominic Trepasso and Rose Timothy Galvin. Their courage and integrity, so clearly evidenced in their unwavering commitment to the poor and oppressed women of Lima, was a "subversive memory" for me as I wrote much of this work. For this I remain deeply grateful to them.

My colleagues and friends in Erie, Pennsylvania, sustained me through the final stages of rewriting this manuscript. They provided the encouragement, affirmation, and necessary social distractions I needed periodically "to keep on keeping on." Warmest thanks go to Jean Kennedy Keck, Fred Keck, Ed Lesser, Mary Hope Wilson, Joy Kronenberger, Tish Donze, Cindy Liotta, Ann Daugherty, Chris Argenziano, and Anne Marie Brault. Finishing this would have been much more difficult without their loving presence in my life.

From time to time I have been privileged to share the joy and struggle of being a Catholic feminist with the community of Erie Benedictines. Their warm hospitality, liturgical integrity, and praxis of peace and justice have been harbingers of hope for me. I thank the entire community for everything they have given me, most especially Mary Louise St. John, Jean Lavin, and Joan Chittister.

My soulmate, colleague, and wise-woman friend, Bernadette Topel, nourished me in so many ways as I wrote these pages. Her presence throughout this process has been pure gift.

Most of all, I thank Curt R. Cadorette. His loving friendship, his deep sensitivity to the issues, and his outrageous patience with my "computer blocks" sustained me beyond measure. In addition, he never once doubted I would write this book!

Finally, to John van Bemmel and Stephen Scharper at Twenty-Third Publications, as well as the many people left unmentioned, my deepest gratitude.

# Contents

## ❡ CHAPTER 5
**Some Implications of Ruether's Christology**     97

# Introduction

As woman and theologian, Rosemary Radford Ruether represents for me the challenge of what it means to be not only white, middle-class, and a U.S. citizen, but also Christian and feminist. My deep respect for the breadth and depth of her work includes the issues she addresses, and how she addresses them. The issues are always complex but she has not been afraid to confront them, and she does this creatively and consistently. Most importantly, a pattern clearly emerges in Ruether's theological agenda and methodology. It is a praxis-based critique that illuminates the inadequacies and limitations of a tradition that encourages oppression rather than redemption and it is always voiced on behalf of the non-dominant peoples of the world.

My purpose in this book is three-fold: (1) to examine the christology of Rosemary Radford Ruether; (2) to present and expound her alternative christological proposal that seeks to narrow the gap between theory and praxis in all christological formulations; and (3) to provide a feminist and liberationist perspective as a resource for criticizing the shortcomings of any traditional or contemporary christology that is oppressive.

In Chapter 1 I present some of Ruether's personal history in order to shed light on how her experiences may have contributed to the way she articulates her christology. Her methodology and biblical hermeneutic are also explained in this chapter, since they illuminate the content and the critique that are characteristic of her theological agenda. Chapters 2 and 3 discuss at length those issues that have given rise to Ruether's christology: anti-Judaism, oppression in Latin and Central America, racism, sexism, and ecological destruction. Chapter 4 places Ruether in a context with other North American theologians who are raising some of the same issues. Chapter 5 outlines some of the implications of Ruether's christological perspective in the areas of methodology, anthropology, soteriology, ecclesiology, ecumenism, and spirituality. Finally, the Epilogue considers some of the strengths and weaknesses of Ruether's christological perspective in light of the ongoing challenge her feminist christology offers to the tradition.

In presenting Ruether's christological concerns, first in regard to the Jews, second from a Third World perspective, third with regard for ecological considerations, and fourth in relation to women, I do not wish to imply that these are disparate developments. On the contrary, it is my opinion that there is both development and integration in Ruether's christology, and that her christology has always issued from a combination of personal and intellectual questions emerging from particular life experiences and from significant personal choices.

Ultimately, Ruether's christological position originates from what has become her lifelong commitment to "...a systematic exploration of the pathologies and redeeming graces of the Christian tradition."[1] In the final analysis, the test of the wisdom and integrity of her christological proposal will not be how well the religious and academic hierarchies applaud her critique and perspective. Rather, the test will be the liberating influence it has on the lives of ordinary Christians victimized by christological formulations that perpetuate sexism, racism, classism, and imperialism.

# ✻ CHAPTER 1

# Personal History and Theological Methodology

In the preface I cited key experiences that profoundly influenced my theological education and perspective on justice. I did this because I have come to believe there is a real connection between one's personal history and the method and content of one's theology. This is certainly true in my life and it is also true, I would claim, in Rosemary Radford Ruether's. A combination of influential people, key historical circumstances, experiences of "social contradiction," "grace," and the personal choices she has made in response to many of these, explain to a great extent her theological questions, concerns, and methodology.[1] In turn, I believe these factors have given direction to her christological agenda and the development it has taken over the course of many years.

## Identifying the Contradictions

*1936-1950: Formative Personal History*
> I grew up in a relatively privileged, patriotic and pious family. Other than my immediate family, most of my relatives on both sides are politically conservative, "genteelly" chauvinist and racist![2]

One might be surprised at a statement like this from feminist theologian Rosemary Radford Ruether. Given these familial roots, Ruether herself is at a loss to explain how she has become who she is. She attributes much to "grace" and her experiences of "social contradiction." I will argue initially, however, that it is more than these two factors that have led her to become the controversial voice that she is. In her early years of development she experienced powerful *personal* experiences of contradiction that help explain not only who she is, but also her theological agenda and methodology.

Ruether's father was a Virginia gentleman, both Anglican and Republican. This quite conservative parent was away a good part of her early life and therefore had relatively little influence upon her development. He died in 1948 when she was only 12. By way of contrast, Ruether's widowed mother Rebecca deeply influenced her. This unusual woman was an English-Austrian Catholic who impressed upon her at an early age that she came from a heroic line of noble and daring adventurers. As a result, Ruether grew up securely self-confident and unafraid to "follow her star."[3]

It is no surprise then that by the time she was eight years old, she was already instinctively rejecting traditional female roles. During her adolescent years, she boasted of having grown up in "a community of mothers and daughters,"[4] where she was encouraged to explore the limitless possibilities of a professional career. I cite this as a fundamental personal experience of contradiction because this was after World War II, the era that gave birth to "the feminine mystique," a time, according to Betty Friedan, when the dream of most women in the United States was

> ...to be perfect wives and mothers. Their highest ambition to have five children and a beautiful house, their only fight to get and keep their husbands. They had no thought for the unfeminine problems of the world outside the home; they wanted the men to make the major decisions. They gloried in their role as women, and wrote proudly on the census blank: "Occupation: housewife.'[5]

Amid this cultural frame of mind, Ruether's mother never left her with the impression that being a wife and mother should be her primary goal in life. This contradictory experience of what was both proper and possible for an American woman in the years following World War II was not the only one she received from her mother.

Mrs. Radford had spent her childhood in Mexico where she developed a deep empathy for working-class women and she often sheltered them in her home.[6] What effect did this have on Rosemary?

> The ability to feel at home with all types of people in many walks of life and levels of wealth and poverty was part of what was communicated to me by her sense of humanity.[7]

Early in her life, then, given her mother's example, Rosemary was taught to question the unconscious chauvinism and racism First World children learn in relation to Third World peoples. It seems Mrs. Radford widely embraced all that was human and tried to teach her daughter to do the same.

A third contradictory experience Ruether had was in relation to Roman Catholicism and ecumenism. Mrs. Radford's Catholicism was "free-spirited and humanistic."[8] Although a devout Catholic, she retained an independent mind toward things ecclesiastical. Rosemary's earliest suspicions of the clerical enterprise were no doubt seeds planted in her mind by a Catholic mother who refused to be intimidated by what she considered to be an often ignorant and narrow-minded clergy.[9]

As a child, Ruether was spared a parochial and ethnically-exclusive version of faith that can be stifling. Instead, she was exposed to theologians from Georgetown in the Jesuit parish she attended with her mother, Carmelite contemplatives who ran a home for the elderly not far from her childhood home, and a private Catholic school education. As she herself has said:

> I grew up assuming that Catholicism was the cloak of a *mysterium tremendum*. When it exhibited a vulgar or narrowly doctrinaire style, I felt assured that it could be safely ignored. I realize now that this is an uncommon experience. American catholics received mostly the fear of the second, little resiliency in the first.[10]

As a young woman, Ruether was also exposed positively to ecumenism. Her mother had many close Protestant women friends who were very interested in religion, which they saw as "the free adventure of the Spirit."[11] These women were products of the feminist movement of the late nineteenth and early twentieth centuries, whose vigor, intellectual curiosity and social concerns upheld them well into their eighties and nineties. Consequently, they had a profound influence on Ruether's initial understanding of what it meant to be a religious woman:

> ...the real heritage upon which I drew was not the official patriarchal heritage but the unofficial matriarchal one. This is the heritage of mothers and daughters who bond together to maintain the survival of the human community while the males are off killing themselves, destroying the world, and stifling the creative spirit with doctrinaire authoritarianism. It is the matriarchal heritage of mothers and daughters that underlies my real life. Perhaps this is why I always instinctively think of God not as the paternal superego, but as the empowering matrix.[12]

Thus, Ruether was exposed through her mother to a healthy view of Catholicism along with a nascent respect for and attraction to ecumenism. As a result, by the time she was ready to enter college at 18 in 1954, she had been nourished on several personal experiences of contradiction, i.e., values that contradicted the reigning ideology of church and culture. These experiences taught her that women were powerful, creative, and strong; that as a woman she could pursue her gifts and talents without apology; that the poor were persons who deserved respect and dignity; that Catholicism could be empowering; that God is the matriarchal Ground of Being; and, that extra-Catholic religious experience is a valuable source of inspiration and truth.

While most male influence on Ruether's development was generally remote, she did have a positive experience of her Uncle David. He was a nurturing man who encouraged her to be creative and exposed her to the arts, music, and dance.[13] This uncle was not a blood relative but one through marriage. Although he was Jewish, Ruether claims he was not directly influential on her work regarding Jewish-Christian relations. However, in some way she does feel her relationship to him made her latently sensitive to the issue. She herself has said:

> Whenever the subject of the Jews was mentioned I seemed

to feel a special pang of personal pathos, as though here
was a mystery that must be explored, a secret that under-
lay some unspoken tragedy of our whole civilization. It is
possible that my uncle helped to create that sensitivity in
an unintended way.[14]

Ruether's Uncle David seems to have offered her two personal experiences of contradiction. He was a nurturing male who affirmed
her talent and intelligence without expecting her, eventually, to
fill a traditional female role; secondly, her relationship with
him, a Jewish man whom she perceived to be uncomfortable with
his origins, predisposed her to be sensitive to Jews and to question
the prevailing assumptions Christians and Christianity had
about them.[15] It is my contention, then, that Ruether's relationship with her Uncle David contributed in some significant way to
her later christological concern with the anti-Judaism that
shapes both the structure and content of traditional christology.

## 1950-1960: Educational Preparation/Marriage

Ruether would be the first to admit that her development was re-
markably influenced by a number of charismatic adults. One of
these was her high school history teacher. Through her word and
example Ruether learned "the evils of American racism."[16] It is to
this teacher that she attributes the seeds that flowered in her a
decade later when she became actively involved in the civil
rights movement. To have been exposed to an educator with the
courage to name the United States as a racist society in the 1950s
was a significant personal experience for Ruether that, again, contradicted the reigning ideology of the day.

After she entered Scripps College at Claremont, California, in
1954, she continued to have the good fortune of being exposed to
teachers who encouraged her to continue this line of questioning.
She refers to her undergraduate and graduate years at Claremont
as "years of dramatic intellectual awakening," "years of conversion," years that cast her into "a process of continual, self-
motivated search for enlarged understanding... ," years that gave
her a bedrock of historical consciousness, particularly that of
Western historical experience.[17] She claims they also imparted to
her a methodological base that to this day undergirds the way
she both asks and answers questions.

It was at this time in her studies that the credibility of Christianity became a question for her. Although she intended to become a Fine Arts major, she found herself studying classical culture and philosophy. Both were springboards for her later studies of the Bible, the origins of Christianity and theology. This intellectual inquiry raised in her a greater awareness of the contradictions inherent in Christianity. Thus, for Ruether, Scripps began what has become "a lifetime of trying to understand and evaluate Western cultural and religious experience."[18]

Under the influence of two classics scholars, particularly Robert Palmer and Philip Merlan, Ruether experienced several kinds of contradictions that challenged her heretofore "elitist and secure" Catholic sensibilities.[19] Palmer, who was of Protestant background, was overtly contemptuous of Christianity, "which he considered a graveyard religion."[20] Nonetheless, it was he who initially taught her to think theologically. Through him she ". . . discovered the meaning of religious symbols, not as extrinsic doctrines, but as living metaphors of human existence."[21] Not only did she receive from him a profoundly critical view of Christianity, but also a deepening of the ecumenical spirit her mother and her mother's friends had engendered in her. Again, such an experience deeply contradicted the reigning ideology of Catholicism in the 1950s.

At age 19 this Catholic woman learned from Palmer that

> All religions begin in theophany, the real encounter with the numinous, present in a particular way in a particular time and place. "God" in this sense is plural: "the gods." Although the underlying reality of the divine may be one, the appearances of the divine are necessarily many and distinct according to different configurations of site, community and historical moment.[22]

Further, Palmer taught her that religious faith was more an existential experience than it was a matter of accepting doctrinal propositions, something that surely contradicted what she had learned from 11 years of Catholic school education.[23]

During her second year at Scripps, Ruether had her first profound "shock," or what she calls "negativity experience" of social contradiction.

The professor mentioned casually that the church did not

oppose slavery or serfdom. In fact, it had condoned it and was itself among the last to give up the ownership of serfs. It is hard to say why this shocked me. I suppose that I just assumed from my American background that slavery would be abhorrent to everyone. The Catholic church must surely have opposed it. I sensed immediately that if the opposite was the case, then this was a massive fact that would fundamentally reshape my whole conception of the authority of the church. A church which continually, for most of its history, accepted and justified slavery was not "infallible" in morals, either in teaching or practice. Most of what I have subsequently learned about the church in the past and today has confirmed that impression.[24]

As a result of this experience, she "set out to find the deeper and more intellectually challenging heritage of Catholicism";[25] one that would firmly contradict the unjust social positions that it held.

In graduate school she studied Martin Luther and Karl Barth, whose contradictory theological views gave her a further framework for criticizing the institutional church. At this time she also began her critique of Augustinian dualism, something that would pervade much of her ongoing critical perspective vis-a-vis the Christian tradition. It was her study of Eastern Orthodoxy, however, with its holistic view of nature, grace, self, and universe that was to remain significant in all that she undertook.[26]

When a junior in college she met Herman Ruether, a graduate student in political science at Claremont. They married a short time after, but not before she made it clear she had "no intention of simply becoming a housewife."[27] He adjusted without much difficulty and she attributes this in large part to the fact that he came from a working-class background where economic survival demanded that both partners share the workload, publicly and privately. Thus, as a young married couple they struggled for a relationship of mutuality—a relationship that contradicted the prevailing role expectations in middle-class marriages in the 1950s.

As a Roman Catholic married woman who refused to accept the traditional role of housewife and mother, Ruether's very being was challenged by the church's position on women. In a deeply personal way she confronted head-on the hiatus between her self-understanding as a strong, capable, intelligent, independent woman and the church's attitude and practice toward women via its position on contraception:

> It was evident to me from the beginning that I did not agree with the position and intended to practice child-planning. But the message of the church became positively menacing toward a young couple in that period of American Catholicism. From all sides I received messages that my salvation lay in a passive acquiescence to God and biological destiny; that any effort to interfere with "nature" was the most heinous crime. Virtually no criticism of this position was culturally available in the world in which I moved at that time.[28]

This personal "negativity experience" was to be fueled later by her insights into the oppressive condition of all married Catholic women, especially those who were poor women of minority groups.[29] It would be the initial catalyst for her ongoing commitment to expose the contradictory ecclesiastical attitudes and practices that oppress and dehumanize women.

### 1960-Present: Theo-Political Integration
Ruether admits that she did not become a social activist until she was about 25 years old; until then her life was "severely academic."[30] This shift, she explains, took place for two reasons. The first is that she was led to read the newspapers more than she previously had, since her husband's field was political science. Secondly, the historical events of the 1960s—the civil rights movement, the Vietnam war movement, Vatican II, and the resurgence of feminism—invaded the university and religious worlds she inhabited.[31]

These years she began to reappropriate and reassess her Catholic Christian identity. Her pre-Vatican II disposition to ecumenism coupled with the *aggiornamento* of the Second Vatican Council provided her with a flexible basis for remaining a Roman Catholic Christian. Also, at this time she belonged to a progressive network of Catholics centered in a monastery which blended the best of Zen Buddhism with the spirit of Benedict, hence nurturing her desire for a religious stance that was both personal and political, contemplative and active, and marked by simplicity without being perversely ascetic.[32]

The mid-1960s was a time of ferment and challenge both in the church and the nation, a time when friendships with people like Thomas Merton and Gregory Baum deeply influenced Ruether. Simultaneously, the Catholic anti-war movement became for her a profound medium for stating what it meant to be both Catholic and a U.S. citizen in terms of social action, theological reflection, and community life.

Her experience in the civil rights movement also deepened and broadened her methodological base and catapulted her into a political consciousness that has proven prophetic. To illustrate this she recalls:

> An important "peak" experience for me was the summer I spent working for civil rights in Mississippi in 1966. Here, for the first time, I learned to look at America from the black side; to see safety in the black community and danger in nightriding whites or white officers of the law.[33]

She has referred to this as "a watershed experience," "a momentous learning experience."[34] In an undeniable way, as a white, middle-class American woman, Ruether learned something of what it means to belong to a racial minority in the United States and the cost to whites who identify with them. Poignantly the contradictions within the U.S. political system were brought home to her as institutionalized racism. This experience impelled her to incorporate a black perspective in the way she "did" theology at Howard University in Washington, D.C., and moved her to explore other related issues that would further reveal the social contradictions in both church and society. Thus, her involvement in the civil rights and peace movements of the 1960s sharpened her perceptions of oppression's myriad faces and crystalized for her their interrelatedness. As she has noted:

> It was not merely a question of racism at home, but racist neo-colonialism and militarism in the relation of rich and poor nations. Intervention abroad bred police repression and bureaucratic paranoia at home. One began to connect the historic structures of oppression: race, class, sex, colonialism, finally the destructive patterns of human society toward nature, in an integrated vision of social contradictions and demands for social revolution.[35]

As her expanding perception of social contradiction took on a global expression she began to rethink the nature of the world she lived in and the ecclesiastical and political institutions she participated in. Ruether named the duplicity and betrayal she found in both "social sin." She describes it as that which "cuts across generations" and is "historically inherited" by individuals who are socialized into roles of domination and oppression and taught that they are correct and normal.[36]

This growing awareness of social sin was brought home to her in a very personal way in 1963, at the time of her daughter's birth. Ruether shared a hospital room with a Mexican-American woman named Assumptione who had just given birth to her ninth child with great difficulty. The doctor urged this weary woman to practice birth control in order to prevent further pregnancies but she resisted his suggestions. Ruether later learned Assumptione felt bound by the Catholic church's teaching against using artificial means of birth control and that she feared her husband's hostility to the idea. Ruether was already personally sensitive to the plight of Mexican-American women through her mother's influence. Assumptione's tragedy became additionally explosive for Ruether, because of her own experience of oppression as a married Catholic woman. Thus, the situation erupted for Ruether into a scathing critique of the church's position on this issue. She explains:

> It was necessary to criticize this policy and the entire sexual ethic and viewpoint on women and marriage that it represented, not just for my own sake, but for those millions of Assumptiones weeping in maternity beds around the world. Only gradually did it become clear that these views themselves were an integral part of a sexist ideology and culture whose purpose was to make women the creatures of biological destiny. This was connected not only with woman's reproductive role, but her work role in the household and society.[37]

In speaking out on this issue, however, Ruether confronted the fundamental issue of this whole debate, the problem not simply of women's reproductive rights, but the problem of clerical versus lay power in the church. Hence, by 1968, with the resurgence of the feminist movement, she would begin to denounce not only clericalism, but also sexism. Together they formed the bases of the oppressive, clerical stranglehold that characterized ecclesiastic attitudes toward lay people in general and toward women in particular. The misogyny Ruether found in the Judeo-Christian tradition she also discovered in society. Denouncing the false anthropology both church and state used (and continues to use) to define women as inferior and secondary human beings, she began to uncover and announce an alternative theological vision. In her research into late antiquity, the Middle Ages, and the seventeenth century to the present, she learned that women have continually emerged from periods of repressive social and ecclesiastical history with a vision of equality. This vision overturned and replaced the androcentric bias running through dominant religious traditions and culture. Her denunciations of sexism, to this day, are accompanied by her fervent avowals of a new vision of a community of mutuality that demands both social and religious reconstruction beyond patriarchy.[38] This critique and vision have been fundamental to the development of her feminist christology.

Ruether's vision of mutuality includes a critique of the structural-economic injustice that characterizes the Third World. It is grounded in her own reality as a citizen of the United States and flows from her personal experience.

One consequence of her involvement in the civil rights and peace movements of the 1960s for example, has been her poignant perception of how deeply interstructured global injustice has become.[39] Outraged at Western hegemony over Third World people and resources, she has questioned the foundations of Western industrial expansion and concluded:

> The same pattern of dependency, exploitation of cheap labor, and colonization of resources—metals, oil, fertile land—continues in more masked forms under neo-colonialism and hides under what is euphemistically called development. The militarization of Western nations, particularly the United States, the policeman of Western colonialism, is inextricably linked with the protection of this empire. This is the reality that lies under the myth of anti-communism and the defense of "democracy."[40]

Also, she has candidly named the United States as "...the center of the neo-colonialist strategy for tying the resources of the globe to the American and European internationalist capitalist system."[41] Furthermore, she has asserted that this appropriation of resources has brutalized the Third World. Her denunciations in this regard have included the myth of U.S. goodness and innocence in the global arena, but have not stopped there.

True to her methodology, Ruether has not simply engaged in negation as the framework for her criticism. Ruether's affirmation of the United States' ideals of justice and freedom for all, forged in the beginning by a people in search of a new humanity, has shed light on what she calls the "non-imperial identity" of the United States, i.e., an identity that is outraged by U.S. actions that diminish justice, peace, and freedom in the world.[42] Thus, Ruether's critique seeks to offer the United States an alternative identity rather than simply painting the U.S. as "the beast."

Her consciousness of these systemic dimensions of global injustice, and the particular role the United States plays in maintaining these injustices, have compelled her to be outspoken in her defense of liberation theology. In turn, liberation theology has challenged her to clarify her understanding of the relationship between theology and politics, as well as the political dimension of biblical messianic faith. Elaborating on this, she has stated:

> Thus, the question is not whether a theology is political or not, but rather what kind of politics it mandates. Only a theology that denounces all forms of impoverishment (including spiritual impoverishment) and calls for a more just and mutual society, as God's mandate for creation, [is] in line with the normative message of biblical hope.[43]

For Christians committed to social justice, and particularly for those concerned about U.S. interventionism in Central and Latin America, Ruether's efforts to integrate theology and politics are harbingers of hope in the ongoing struggle against global injustice.

## From Contradictions to Dialectics: Naming the Methodology

*Dialectical and Biblical Foundations*
Ruether's personal and social experiences of contradiction prepared her to develop, over the course of many years, a creative and challenging way of "doing theology," that is, her methodolo-

gy. Given her personal history and intellectual journey, she is no stranger to ambiguity, nuance or the dangers of oversimplification. The realities of the human condition have remained for her ever complex and often contradictory.

Thus she has constructed a methodology that is dialectical, one that she believes does justice to her search for truths that will set us all free.[44]

Ruether claims she began to think dialectically long before she read the Hegelians, but she does not elaborate on why or how. She states that in her undergraduate studies of the clash between the worlds of classical antiquity and biblical faith she became suspicious of any idea that appeared to be dualistic.[45] She insists that this kind of "oppositional thinking" has been the nemesis of Western thought in relations between Christians and Jews, Christians and pagans, Protestants and Catholics. By way of contrast, Ruether takes traditional polarities—male/female, soul/body, humankind/nature, transcendent/historical—and seeks to transform them into dynamic unities.

She does this by negation and affirmation, i.e., by "an exploration of the repressed 'other side' in order to move beyond both poles to a new synthesis that could include them both. . . in a new way."[46] Using negation in order to affirm, she sees the former "not as an attack on someone else's person or community, but as a self-criticism of the distortion of one's own being and community."[47] Criticism understood in this way makes reconstruction and liberation possible only through this "cross of negation."[48] The latter affirmation demands, "both theoretical struggles against false ideologies of oppression and practical struggle against its social consequences."[49] This dialectical stance seeks to uncover the truer self in persons and communities and thereby to move beyond the alienation created by oppositional thinking and head toward a new vision of wholeness, mutuality, and justice.[50]

Prescinding from an "objective" approach to scholarship, Ruether's dialectical methodology and theological agenda spring from her Christian commitment. They are reflections of her faith in the goodness of creation, in a just and compassionate God and in the capacity of human beings to repent and be changed so that the Kingdom might come on this earth. They also reflect her deep sensitivity to the complexity of the human condition, flawed as it is by evil and sin. For Ruether, "faith must cease to be an intellectual affirmation about some 'purely spiritual' matter, and must become incarnate in work and action."[51]

She expresses this conviction methodologically (1) by always situating a particular instance of injustice she is attending to within the interconnecting contexts of sex, class, race, and economic structures; (2) by grounding her method in the biblical prophetic-messianic tradition, and, more recently, (3) by urging the development of "a new body of midrashim."[52]  In her own words:

> This means...that I relate the critique of social pathology and the lifting up of social alternatives to the biblical prophetic-messianic tradition. The biblical heritage. . . is a way of grounding the whole struggle in order to give it both greater faith and endurance and better resources to criticize its own pathology than would be the case with secular social analysis.[53]

Thus her method has biblical, dialectical, and experiential foundations.

Ruether's use of the prophetic-messianic tradition in her methodology is an outgrowth of her study of the messianic idea in antiquity. She claims the origin of this concept lies in the ancient kingship ideology of Egypt, Babylonia, and Canaan, which, in a yearly cultic festival, celebrated the death and regeneration of the cosmic, political, and natural orders. This in turn was adapted by the Hebrew temple cult in what became the annual New Year's festival, i.e., the celebration of Yahweh's enthronement and the establishment of Yahweh's reign. The mood of this "Day of the Lord" was ecstatic and exultant as it anticipated the transformation and transfiguration of the world in peace, justice and material abundance.[54]

The eighth-century prophets shifted the focus of this cultic celebration from the hope for nationalistic vindication to an insistence on personal and social conversion. Such a shift demanded the moral purification of Israel, meaning repentance within the nation if it were ever to experience peace, prosperity, and national autonomy again.[55]

> It was Amos particularly that made a devastating reversal of the traditional celebration of the "Day of the Lord" (i.e., the cultic celebration of the establishment of Yahweh's Reign) by proclaiming that this "Day," contrary to

naive expectations of the people, will not be one of blessing, but one of wrath and judgment, in vindication of a righteousness which belongs not automatically to the people but to God alone.[56]

Thus the early prophets interpret Israel's covenantal relationship with Yahweh in historical and ethical terms while stressing the judgmental side of Yahweh's covenant with Israel. In addition, they criticize Israel's naive nationalism along with its religious leadership and rituals insofar as they avoid the concrete demands for justice in the social order. Once Israel's religious consciousness is awakened by the ethical demands of the covenant, and once it struggles to incorporate religious and social reforms into its self-understanding, the prophetic pattern of judgment develops to include the promise of redemption and salvation as well as that of wrath and judgment. A prophetic vision of fulfillment— nationally, religiously, socially and economically—is offered to Israel as a coming future historical eon which will arrive when Israel meets Yahweh's demands for justice, righteousness and fidelity. Consequently, "the prophets have turned the cultic pattern of gratuitous distress and gratuitous renewal into an ethical pattern of judgment and redemption based on repentance."[57]

This prophetic critique of religion and society exposes the deepest meaning of the "Word of God" for Ruether because this dialectic (the denunciation or judgment of Israel's sinfulness along with the affirmation or promise of its salvation through conversion) retrieves the prophetic meaning of language from its ideological deformations. That is to say, the prophetic word is spoken on behalf of the poor and oppressed rather than in favor of the ruling classes who seek to maintain their power and privilege within the status quo. In the final analysis, when this prophetic critique is faithfully applied, it prevents religion not only from becoming a tool in the hands of the dominant social and religious powerbrokers, but also from becoming a platform for revenge in the hands of the oppressed.[58]

As Ruether explains it, the structure of prophetic thought itself is dialectical. On the one hand it *denounces* sin and apostasy by expressing divine wrath and judgment; on the other hand it *announces* the promise of salvation through renewed faith and conversion.[59]

At its best, prophetic faith represents a decisive break with the pattern of religion that makes the divine a conforming theophany of the existing social order. Instead, the existing social order as a hierarchy of rich over poor, the powerful over the weak, is seen as contrary to God's will, and apostasy to God's intent for creational community. The revelation of God therefore appears as judgment against this apostate order. God comes as an advocate of the oppressed, overturner of an unjust order, whose action in history points forward to a reconstructed community that will fulfill God's intent for creation, a time when God's will shall be "done on earth as it is in heaven."[60]

Methodologically, then, biblical prophetic criticism becomes Ruether's way of protesting against the established order and also of pointing toward new possibilities for community through a transformation of values.

In conjunction with this prophetic criticism, Ruether incorporates the messianic tradition into her methodological critique of church and culture. In this context, the messianic tradition means hope, i.e., "the hope for salvation in a total social and historical sense."[61] It is not merely a religious idea but also a political one. It is both a historical and transcendent anticipation of the coming of the Kingdom. As such, it expects God's will to be done on earth concretely through the overcoming of all unjust, exploitative relationships. Messianic hope exposes the chasm between what is and what ought to be and demands participation in the struggle to eliminate oppression as the only credible response of obedience to God.[62]

According to Ruether, Jesus, as the messianic prophet, is the paradigmatic embodiment of this hope. As such, he denounces the political and religious leaders of his day who lust after power, prestige, and wealth only to lord it over the defenseless. Simultaneously, to those without hope, those oppressed and denigrated by the unjust social structures of his day, Jesus brings the promise of salvation. The latter will overturn the system of status created by wealth, rank, education and religious observance. Thus the new era of justice Jesus envisages will transform all social structures that keep people in oppressive relationships with one another[63] Prophetic criticism and messianic hope, then, exist, for Ruether, as "principles of discernment by which the shortcomings of the present community are judged."[64]

Ruether's methodology is rooted in the belief that the biblical prophetic-messianic tradition contains liberating elements that point to the true vision of community God intended for all people. For her this tradition reveals, in its dialectic of judgment and promise, that the sin and apostasy that create unjust social relations are to be negated, while what promotes authentic community—peace, justice, mutuality—is to be affirmed. This tradition, according to Ruether, also challenges us to see the gap between what is and what should be. It denies a totally "other-worldly" view of redemption and calls us, as historical agents, to make the Kingdom come as much as possible on this earth.

## A Feminist Recontextualization

As her use of the prophetic-messianic tradition illustrates, Ruether affirms the value of many biblical texts as a positive resource for feminist theology. In addition, she refutes the claim that there is no positive continuity between feminist theology and biblical traditions. Nor does she support the stance that Scripture is "hopelessly" patriarchal. She does insist, however, that despite the liberating dynamic present in many texts, Scripture remains thoroughly androcentric. This dynamic is *not* expressed from the perspective of oppressed women. Even the New Testament accounts of marginalized women are presented from a male point of view.

Building on her previous work, then, Ruether offers four steps for a feminist critique and revision of any given religious tradition: (1) to carefully analyze the elements of a particular religious tradition, which appear to be positive for women, for their androcentric biases; (2) to determine how the stories and symbols taken from past religious traditions can be transformed from an androcentric perspective into one that is liberating for women; (3) to decide at what point we need to transcend reinterpretation of past traditions and develop a generation of new stories, symbols, and rituals derived from women's experience; this step includes determining the norms by which we will be able to discern which new stories, symbols, and rituals promote wholeness rather than destruction; (4) to determine whether such feminist restatements of past traditions should proceed independently of one another, or rather, whether feminists involved in this process of critique and revision can begin to unite around some new synthesis of the perspectives previously at odds with one another.[65]

Ruether applies these four steps of revision and critique to the Christian interpretation of biblical religion. Acknowledging Christian indebtedness to the Jewish religious tradition embodied in the Hebrew Scriptures, she focuses on the distinctive expressions of religion found there. Negatively, she names these as the patriarchal ordering of society, the patriarchal imaging of God and of monotheism. She claims monotheism strenghtened patriarchalism since it presupposed a male deity and therefore the hierarchy of male over female. However, Ruether maintains that since one can also find female imagery in the Hebrew Scriptures, monotheism left open the possibility that the one God transcended gender-role stereotyping.[66]

The most distinctive element Ruether finds in Hebrew religion is the shift from mythically- to historically-rooted religion. Such a movement, according to her, functions as an impetus to historical action. "Historical precedent becomes ethical paradigm for living historically in community."[67] In addition to this historical shift, Ruether also finds a social shift in the function of religion within the Hebrew faith. She argues that this social shift is evidenced in the prophetic critique of religion as sacralizing existing systems of power and wealth at the expense of the poor and oppressed. Such a shift, to her mind, provides the foundational language of social criticism and historical transformation in culture which has its roots in the Bible. This prophetic paradigm is found in both the Hebrew and Christian Scriptures. It not only denounces an unjust and oppressive use of power in society, but also the use of religion to confirm such oppressive power. Such a critique of religion is self-criticism, which according to Ruether, "...aims at the renewal of the ethical content of religious practice."[68]

> The prophetic paradigm also contains the language of radical social transformation. God is seen as active in history overthrowing oppressors, bringing into being a new social order of justice and mercy. Hope is directed toward a historical future where the wrongs of the present system will be righted.[69]

No doubt this paradigm, if taken seriously, can be a source of liberation for all the poor and oppressed.

For Ruether, then, feminism is a restatement of the prophetic paradigm in a modern form and is made in the context of women's oppression and hope for liberation. Women, too, cry out against oppression and stand in judgment of religious systems that justify it. But unlike ancient Hebrew prophecy, feminism decries the patriarchal oppression of women and envisions the liberation of women. The Hebrew prophets' critique remained confined to the concerns of oppressed males in an oppressed nation vis a vis the powerful males of the society or the imperial powers that surrounded Israel. Although it might seek to alleviate the oppression of slaves or women in the patriarchal family, prophetic critique did not originate from these groups nor did it express a consciousness of patriarchy itself as contrary to nature or God's will. Thus, according to Ruether, feminism can appropriate the prophetic-messianic paradigm and claim it as its source only by radical recontextualization. "[Feminism] applies the language of critique of oppression and of oppressive religion, and the language of future hope to questions of patriarchy and the liberation of women; these were not addressed by the ancient authors."[70]

Ruether calls this application of biblical prophetic language to modern issues "analogical midrash." It is not historical exegesis but rather "the retelling of ancient paradigms in the context of modern issues and modern consciousness."[71] Ruether cautions feminists to be very clear when applying the language about oppression and liberation to patriarchy and to women, since they are not exegeting the text, but rather retelling the story in a new way. "Feminist hermeneutics thus claims the power to retell the story in new ways."[72] Thus, a contemporary feminist liberation midrash discerns the liberationist intention in the biblical story and recontextualizes that liberationist element in the context of women's experience of suffering and oppression today.[73]

A second way of retelling traditional stories from the perspective of a contemporary feminist liberation midrash is to reverse the specifically misogynist intention of the story and thereby release the power of women that the old story represses. Ruether cites Judith Plaskow's retelling of the story of Lilith as "a brilliant example of this type of midrash."[74]

A third approach is to tell new stories that appropriate women's primary religious experiences. Ruether refers to this as "revelation." In her own words:

> I believe...that revelation, in the sense of primary religious vision, happens today and is not confined to some privileged period of the past. This is another way of saying, theologically, that the Holy Spirit is present and is not simply the tool of historical institutional structures limited to the past.[75]

She points out that although most of these primary visions remain private, some are becoming new communal paradigms. One such new paradigm is the image of the Christa or crucified woman.[76] The example she gives to illustrate this is a story told by one of her students:

> One woman recounted her experience of being raped in a woods. During the rape she became convinced that she would be killed and resigned herself to her impending death. When the rapist finally fled, and she found herself still alive, she experienced a vision of Christ as a crucified woman. This vision filled her with relief and healing. "I would not have to explain to a male God that I had been raped. God knew what it was like to be a woman who had been raped."[77]

For Ruether this story dramatizes a deep appropriation of women's sufferings in terms of a primary religious vision. Like all primary religious visions, she argues that this story transcends mere interpretation or theological restatement. It arises from a depth of previously unarticulated female experience and discloses many levels of meaning. Further, she insists:

> ...what is stated most primarily in this vision is that the divine is present where the divine has never been allowed to be present in patriarchal religion, in female sexual victimization by men. The divine is present here, not as representative of the male who is the victimizer, but on the side of the female victim, one with the female victim, one who knows this anguish, who is a part of it, and who also heals and empowers women to rise from the dead, to be recreated beyond and outside the grasp of this negative power.[78]

Ruether maintains that it is the power of women gathering together that has enabled them to do feminist midrash. "Here women not only claim the right to preach, i.e., to interpret traditional texts. They claim the right to write the texts, to generate the symbols and stories out of their own religious experience."[79] Such a movement is taking place among Christian, Jewish, and neo-pagan feminists. Despite their differences, Ruether argues, biblically-based Jewish and Christian feminists are able to incorporate various contributions of neo-pagan feminists into their own theological and liturgical work. Such Jewish and Christian feminists, "stand on a boundary, facing two directions and refuse to opt simply for one against the other."[80] Simultaneously, their dialectical stance enables them to affirm the essential liberationist message of their historical/biblical traditions while negating the patriarchal oppression which also characterizes these same traditions. In addition, these Jewish and Christian feminists are open to new possibilities, especially those generated by the primary religious experience and imagination of women.

> Perhaps what is in the process of being born through this dialectic is a feminist resynthesis of the various layers of the religious tradition itself. Such a resynthesis is looking for an integration of religion based on mimetic experiencing of the rhythms of nature; of religion shaped by historical responsibility and the striving of obedience to law in order to create a just society, and finally, of religion shaped by ecstatic encounter with redemption from historical ambiguity and a proleptic entrance into the blessedness of harmonious integration of human history and nature.[81]

According to Ruether, feminist theology is already engaged in this dynamic resynthesis, evident in the spontaneous interaction among Jewish, Christian and neo-pagan feminist communities in the cyclic, historical and eschatological dimensions of their religious traditions. However, she urges us to become more consciously reflective and theological about this process in order to better understand our accountability to the past, to each other, and to a just and healthy future for all of creation.[82]

*Critical Considerations*
Ruether's call for the development of a new body of midrashim, rooted as it is in women's experience of oppression and suffering,

can have a profound impact on contemporary christological perspectives for five reasons:

1) Contrary to most christological formulations, it presupposes the value and integrity of women and women's experience.

2) It denounces the androcentrism that pervades the Scriptures and much scriptural interpretation.

3) By recontextualizing the prophetic paradigm in the context of women's experience of suffering and oppression, it expands the liberating dynamic within the Scriptures and renews the meaning of the prophetic-messianic tradition itself. Jesus would be understood anew in this context, i.e., as one who sought healing and wholeness for all, women and men.

4) It celebrates and affirms women's experience of Christ and deepens our understanding of the infinite presence of the divine in history and *her* story.

5) It invites Jewish, Christian and neo-pagan feminists to join in solidarity against oppression, i.e., patriarchy, offering hope to all who work to promote interreligious dialogue through a renewed christological perspective.

Feminist biblical scholar Elisabeth Schüssler Fiorenza has criticized Ruether's methodology in her feminist critique of the Bible.[83] Schüssler Fiorenza argues that Ruether's use of the prophetic-messianic tradition as a critical, liberating tradition has neo-orthodox implications. By this she means that Ruether uses these traditions in an abstract, idealized, and ahistorical way. She claims that Ruether does this by overlooking the "oppressive androcentric elements of these traditions," and by painting an exclusivist portrait of Christianity over against post-biblical feminist objections to the Scriptures.[84]

In response to Schüssler Fiorenza's criticisms Ruether has clarified her position. She rejects the argument that there are neo-orthodox implications to her method. Rather, she argues that she has tried to illustrate in her methodology "a certain liberating 'dynamic' which is expressed in the prophetic-messianic tradition, and...in secular form, in modern liberation movements."[85] This liberating dynamic, for Ruether, is neither timeless, pure, nor ahistorical. "Rather this liberating dynamic only exists in and as the historical experience of communities engaged in liberating *praxis*."[86] Further, the common elements that characterize this liberating dynamic remain prototypical rather than archetypal for Ruether and she acknowledges them to be particular to a specific cultural context.[87]

Given all this, Ruether makes it very clear that she is not denying that extra-Christian and post-Christian religious cultures can be loci for the revelation of God. She merely objects to any "reversed exclusivism" that would consign the Scriptures to being hopelessly patriarchal, or which would place Goddess feminist spirituality beyond the need for any internal self-critique from a gender- and class-based perspective. She has pointed out both the limitations and possibilities of the liberating dynamic in concrete historical movements and insists it remains a resource for ever new liberating visions and praxis.[88]

In the final analysis Ruether believes both she and Schüssler Fiorenza are talking about the same thing, i.e., "community-based experience in historical social contexts."[89] The task that remains, according to Ruether, is the unrelenting effort to imaginatively reconstruct the social contexts of historical Christianity in such ways that they will be emancipatory for women in both vision and praxis.

No doubt further dialogue between the two feminist scholars will be required as both continue their efforts to liberate women from the stranglehold of patriarchy.

*Implications for Christology*
Ruether's theological methodology, with its dialectical, biblical, and experiential foundations, has several important implications for christology. Some of these are that:

Christians in general and theologians in particular recognize the influence of personal history in the appropriation of a christological perspective, particularly when that history and perspective reflect a sexist, racist, classist or imperialistic view of Christ.

Oppositional or dualistic thinking in any christological formulation should be named and repudiated.

As Christians, we deepen our capacity for self-criticism in the development of christology; also, we see this self-criticism not as an attack on others, but as a way to acknowledge the distortions within ourselves and our own communities.

Traditional polarities, e.g., male/female, soul/body, humankind/nature, transcendent/historical, should be seen dialectically to insure that christology is done from the perspective that neither polarity is superior or inferior to the other. What this could mean for christological reinterpretation is the recognition of women, bodily existence, nature and history as credible witnesses to and sources for understanding Christ. Consequently, all these aspects of reality should be seen as part of a process of ongoing revelation. This, in turn could lead to a more critical and liberating appropriation of the Scriptures, tradition and contemporary human experience as the sources of christology, leading to a transformation of institutionalized patterns of relating in both church and society.

The prophetic-messianic tradition should be a key critical principal of the Bible, enabling the Christian community to evaluate "in new contexts, what is truly the liberating Word of God," with regard to all who have been and continue to be dehumanized by oppressive christological formulations.[90]

The voices of those silenced by past christological formulations—women, Third World peoples, members of other faith traditions, the poor, racial minorities—should be heard, in keeping with Ruether's interpretation of the prophetic critique. Ruether's critique is that which "is in a constant state of revision by situating itself in contemporary issues. . . and by becoming a vehicle for the critical consciousness of groups who have been shut out of the social dialogue in the past."[91]

Ruether's christology thus requires ongoing involvement in the struggle for liberation from everything that promotes dehumanization, particularly patriarchy.

# Questions for Reflection and Discussion

1. Do you agree or disagree with the statement that "there is a real connection between one's personal history and the method and content of one's theology?" Explain.

2. Can you identify with any of Ruether's personal or social experiences of contradiction in your own growth process as a religious person?

3. Reflect on Ruether's definition of social sin. Discuss its implications for morality today.

4. Ruether's methodology (the way she does theology) incorporates biblical, dialectical, and experiential aspects. Explain each of these.

5. What is the prophetic-messianic tradition and, according to Ruether, how can it be liberating for women?

6. Do you agree or disagree with Ruether's perspective on revelation? Explain.

7. Discuss Ruether's suggestion that the Christa or crucified woman is a new communal paradigm or model of Christ. What are the implications of this for women? For men?

# ✻ CHAPTER 2

# The Christology of Rosemary Radford Ruether: Judaism and the Christological Tradition

## Introduction

Ruether's christology issues from theoretical concerns about and practical involvement in the struggle to comprehend the meaning of Jesus in a divided world. Initially she pursued these concerns by writing about the origins of christology in Judaism and early Christianity. Her research led her to a discovery of denigrating attitudes of the church fathers toward both women and Jews. By 1974 she had edited and authored two books dealing with these issues, which, along with her previous work, laid a strong foundation for her developing christological perspective.[1] This perspective was to continue to develop under several influences, not the least of which was her participation in the political movements of the late 1960s and early 1970s. The 1970s also found her increasingly responsive to the issues raised by Third World liberation theologians, especially their understanding of the historical Jesus.

I have also suggested that her broad-minded and vibrant Catholic mother, her gentle and nurturing Jewish uncle, two particular college professors who taught her as an undergraduate, and the Second Vatican Council, were other significant influences on the development of her christology.

In response to a question I asked her regarding the scholarly influences on her christological development, Ruether informed me that there are:

> None. I developed my christology by studying the ancient sources and the development of the idea of Messiah/ Christianity in antiquity, not from modern theologians.[2]

Ruether's experience as a woman of faith, a social activist, and an academic have enabled her to perceive how injustice is structured on local, national, and global levels. This perspective is the result of her efforts to understand the suffering of those most victimized in this world. This has meant a critique not only of the economic and socio-political structures that promote oppression, but also of those patterns in theology that have victimized people because of their sex, race, or religious affiliation.[3] As a result she has become keenly sensitive to christological formulations articulated from a white, Western, male, and middle-class perspective. Too often these are not only sexist and racist, but also blatantly imperialistic and classist.

It is my suggestion that all of these factors have combined to create a framework from which Ruether proposes a christology. Her christology is not only *proleptic* (anticipating the fullness of Jesus' messianic identity yet to be revealed) and *paradigmatic* (relative to Christians as a particular historical community), but also countercultural and historically renewable in every age. In the following pages, I attempt to develop her christology in a more detailed and concrete manner.

## Judaism and Christology

*Hebraic Messianism*
The historical development of Hebraic messianism and the political connotations accompanying that development are central to Ruether's christological perspective. She maintains that Jewish messianism and prophetic futurism developed into apocalypticism and eschatology in a process deeply influenced by a Near

Eastern cultural context.[4] In the course of this process, apocalyptic thought tended to differentiate the messianic (historical) era from the eschatological era. The messianic era is generally understood as a period in history when the Messiah will come while the eschatological era refers to that period of life after death. The important issue for Ruether's christology here is that the historical and eschatological eras are distinguished. She points out:

> ...the Messiah is *never* associated with the eschatological redemption. The eschatological age is thought of as the direct reign of God. This is true of the New Testament book of Revelation, where Christ reigns over the millennium, not over the eternal new Jerusalem. Thus the basically political meaning of the Messiah is not only maintained, but reasserts itself in the apocalyptic development.[5]

Consequently, the idea of the Messiah within the developing context of Hebraic messianism is always and only a political figure whose historical role is to assume the kingship of Israel. The following, then, is a brief attempt to highlight the significant features that combined historically and politically to shape Hebraic messianism and the material hope to which it gave birth.

As mentioned above, the origin of Jewish messianism and the messianic idea is the ancient kingship ideology of Egypt, Babylonia, and Canaan. The king was the main spokesperson in this public cult, and mediator with Yahweh for national salvation on both a social and natural plane. Such mediation occurred during the celebration of the "Day of the Lord" where all of Israel's future hopes were renewed.[6]

The eighth-century prophets criticized this cultic celebration for its emphasis on "national security" and self-aggrandizement, rather than on Israel's need for personal and social repentance. Once Israel began to heed the demands of the prophets for moral renewal, the latter became an essential ingredient in its self-understanding and a recognized pre-condition for its future welfare. This concept of Jewish messianism and the hope it engendered continued to grow and expand under the prophets, particularly in the post-exilic period where it came under Iranian, Chaldean, and Greek influences. The latter reshaped its language so that it became both apocalyptic and eschatological. This development is clearly seen in the Jewish apocalyptic writings of the Hellenistic period, that period in Jewish history of militant resistance against Greek and Roman imperialism.[7]

> In this resistance struggle it was ancient Jewish messianism, in increasingly radicalized form, that served as the ideology of the freedom fighters. We cannot understand either this period of Jewish history or its connection with the birth of Christianity unless it is clear that Jewish messianism was a zealot creed.[8]

Thus, Jewish messianism was both religious and political. The modern dualism between religion and politics was foreign to the Hebrew worldview because "for Judaism religion was the 'politics of God.'"[9] Even as the understanding of the Kingdom became more transcendentalized, more "other worldly," this did not preclude a unity between religion and politics; rather, it implied a greater radicalization of the two. As a result, the human condition was seen in more radical terms. Israel came to understand the cosmic dimension of evil and how it pervaded the universe. Thus, there was the realization of the need to overthrow the present system, not just to vindicate Israel, but also to overcome the diabolic forces that had come to control the entire universe.[10]

> Thus transcendental language or language about "another world" is essentially "ought" language in Hebrew thought. The "new world" becomes seen in more radically "other" terms precisely to the degree that the distance between the "ought" and the "is" is seen as deep seated and fundamental. Nevertheless the "other world" is never really some completely unrelated world to the present creation, but rather is always a vision of this present world "renewed"; i.e., this present world remade so that it appears as it "ought to be."[11]

Consequently, from an apocalyptic perspective, the present political order was merely a manifestation of deeper ethical and cosmological aberrations that had to be eliminated before the world could exist as it should. Such a view of a transcendentalized Kingdom, therefore, only underscored how radical—rather than how de-politicized or spiritualized—the apocalyptic understanding of the messianic age had become.[12]

Another significant point in the growth and development of Hebraic messianism is found in the break between prophetic futurism and the apocalyptic worldview found in the book of Daniel. There, historical future hope is transformed into eschatology:

> In this book messianism takes a new leap in its development and promulgates the idea of a resurrection from the dead, thus making the future era not only historical, but eschatological by including the dead from past generations in the future era of judgment and blessedness....[13]

Also, the "Son of Man" figure found in the book of Daniel becomes more of a transcendent messianic figure rather than a restored Davidic king. Ruether cautions, however, that Daniel's "Son of Man" is not a supernatural being, but rather "the 'head' of the people, an archetype and a collective symbol... projected to an ideal future."[14] As such, she insists that the figure is basically eschatological.

The idea of the messianic Kingdom undergoes several changes beyond those proposed by Daniel. In the apocalyptic writings of the second century B.C.E., a dualistic distinction emerges between the present temporal order and the future order of the Kingdom. Since this development is by no means linear and consistent, it does result in what Ruether calls a "double scenario", i.e., "... a blessed messianic age of temporal duration, followed by an end of the world and an eternal eschatological kingdom of the resurrection of the dead."[15] In the apocalyptic literature of the first century B.C.E. the primary pattern in the development of the idea of the messianic Kingdom remains the hope of prophetic futurism, i.e., the hope for a transformed future historical order of infinite blessedness. The resurrection of the dead is sometimes but not always included in this concept.[16]

By the first century C.E. apocalyptic literature developed more systematically to the point where the "end of the world" divides the temporal Kingdom of prophetic futurism from the "new creation," the eschatological and eternal Kingdom of resurrected life. Thus:

> It was the growing tendency in later apocalyptic thought to borrow the Greek metaphysical dualism between mutable Becoming and immutable Being that forced the old Jewish concept of the future kingdom, that was expected to

literally happen in history, into a framework where this transcendence was conceived of as a totally "other world," eternal and immutable, in comparison with the present finite creation.[17]

As a result of this development, Jewish prophetic futurism became a dualistic and eschatological idea about two worlds: one temporal, evil, and beyond redemption; the other eternal, spiritual, and beyond creation. This distinction led to the collapse of the original intent of messianic hope as the historical redemption of the created world. What followed, as a result, was its unfortunate replacement by mysticism and gnosticism.[18]

A key concept for understanding Hebraic messianism is that of the Messiah who "from first to last. . . remains fundamentally a political figure, a future king of Israel."[19] In its most original meaning the term actually referred to the reigning Davidic king. After the fall of the monarchy, however, it was the hope-filled expression for a restored Davidic king whose restoration would include renewed national autonomy. Significantly, it is in the royal psalms that the term "Messiah" appeared and was used as the title most characteristic of the reigning king.[20]

This king was understood to be both the servant of Yahweh and the representative of the people in their relationship to Yahweh. He was a uniquely chosen "son" of God, sharing in Yahweh's sovereignty, and thereby assured of victory over enemies, prosperity, and righteousness. He also expressed the nature of Yahweh in his role as champion of the poor and oppressed. Symbolically, the king was seen to take his place at God's right hand because of this unique mediating relationship, a relationship that did not, however, make him divine. Any references to the king as God are ways of acknowledging his role as both mediator and representative of the benefits that flow to the people from the establishment of the reign of Yahweh.[21] Thus, in times of distress and redemption the king also represented the collective "I" of the people and it was this collective, filial relationship that most significantly makes the king God's "Son" and "Anointed One."[22] However:

As the cultic pattern of renewed life provides the language of historical future hopes, and historical future hope, in turn, becomes increasingly apocalyptic, we also have a corresponding development of royal ideology into a figure of a future "Messiah."[23]

This development is due primarily to Israel's ongoing historical experience of disappointment in the reigning king's failure to live up to his role expectations. Thus Israel shifted its hope to a future ideal king, "a man truly after the Lord's heart whose uprightness would truly be the basis for a time of favor to God's people."[24]

Given the distortions that will later occur in christology's use of messianism, Ruether emphasizes the historical character of Israel's expected Messiah.

> The term "Messiah" becomes a strictly future figure only with the fall of the actual monarchy. With the disappearance of autonomous national life with a reigning Davidic king, all the hopes associated with the king and the national cult were then projected into a hope for a future era of restoration, when the king and the national cult would be reestablished. Yet this future Messiah of the post-exilic prophets is not a trans-historical figure, but rather he is simply a restored Davidic king of a restored national government, even though this hope for restoration might be couched in all the exalted language derived from the old national cult.[25]

As such, the Messiah is the restored monarch representing renewed national power and strength. He is a central symbol of the coming of the Kingdom when the prophets stressed the political and national aspects of Israel's future hope. By way of contrast, however, when the cosmic and ethical aspects of Israel's future hope were being emphasized, manifested in prophetic language about a new creation and a new people with a repentant heart, the stress shifted to the very core of Israel's future hope, namely, the coming of Yahweh's reign. As a result, it is important to recognize that the coming of a messianic person was but *one* expression of this fuller messianic hope for the coming of Yahweh who would order all reality into right relationship with himself.[26]

It is in the Jewish apocalyptic writings (c.170 B.C.E. to C.E. 130) that the word "Messiah" takes on several new connotations. The term begins to refer to a future king of a transcendent Kingdom, a soteriologically active figure, and a warrior who defeats Yahweh's enemies in battle. Earlier this second role belonged to Yahweh alone. And while Yahweh remained the one responsible for ushering in the Kingdom as its judge, the Messiah in apocalyptic biblical literature begins to join Yahweh in this task of judgment, ever remaining but one expression of Yahweh's reign, not its total embodiment. It is important to note, as Ruether points out, that in these writings the soteriological function of the Messiah is in no way connected with his personal suffering or moral accomplishments.[27]

In the later apocalyptic literature of the Zealots (c. C.E. 6-73), the Messiah is characterized as a cosmic warrior who destroys the evil powers of the world in apocalyptic battle.[28]

> The actual historical experience of oppression, first under the Seleucids, and then under the Romans, sparked a movement of messianically inspired guerilla bands, who pictured the Messiah as an apocalyptic warrior in the manner of the glorified memory of the Maccabean victory. Thus the picturing of the Messiah as a warrior must be seen essentially as zealot literature; if not directly written by a zealot "party," at least inspired by an image of national liberation through uprisings of inspired guerilla bands, where the sword, as much as the Torah, becomes the means to the kingdom.[29]

This apocalyptic ferment heightened around the ideal of a coming Messiah roughly a century before and after the birth of Jesus, and occurred as a result of three centuries of Jewish struggle against imperialist powers. The "expected one"—when he actually appeared in history—never totally fulfilled all Jewish messianic expectations and was therefore declared false. This rejection included Jesus as well. Consequently, the Jewish rejection of Jesus as the Messiah should not be understood as Jewish abandonment of religious faith, but rather as Jewish fidelity to its own messianic hope.[30]

*Jesus and Messianism*
From the time of the Maccabees to the Jewish Wars (early second century B.C.E. to C.E. 67-73), several popular messianic movements arose keeping apocalyptic hopes alive, (for example, the Zealots, Prophets, Baptists, Essenes, etc.). It was in this context of messianic and apocalyptic ferment that the Jesus movement arose in Palestine. Galilee, specifically, was a region known for its stridency

toward the Jews of Judea, its anti-legalistic tendencies, especially among the poorer classes, its keen nationalism and antipathy to Jewish rulers as puppets of the Roman authorities, and its volatile messianic faith vulnerable to charismatic personalities.[31] Ruether sees Jesus as falling credibly within this kind of Galilean Judaism because he was a charismatic, a popular preacher, a miracle worker, an exorcist, and an apocalypticist. He was also an anti-legalist who denounced that strict Pharisaism that closed the Kingdom of God to the poor.[32]

With this background, it is understandable why Jesus and his followers—coming to Jerusalem at Passover, and preaching imminent messianic fulfillment—would be seen by the religious and political leaders as a group of dissidents. Like other messianic prophets before him, Jesus preached the apocalyptic inbreaking of the reign of God. His call for repentance and conversion, while predominantly religious, also had cosmic and political implications. The coming of God's reign always implied, among other things, restored political autonomy for Israel and an end to imperialism.[33] Thus:

> We must be clear that the very preaching of the kingdom of God inescapably implied this political consequence, no matter how "transcendentally" the process might be conceived...There is no tradition of messianism in Judaism...which does not have this hope as an intrinsic part of its message...In Jesus' cultural context, to proclaim the imminence of the kingdom of God was a political statement...Neither Jesus nor his audience would have been able to understand how the kingdom could come, while leaving the outward reign of the "evil nations" untouched.[34]

In this context, Ruether maintains that it is the "future Son of Man" sayings that most faithfully preserve Jesus' "messianic consciousness" in relation to his own messianic preaching as well as that of the coming Messiah and the reign of God. She claims Jesus distinguished himself from the coming Son of Man, while maintaining with him a unity of intention. Those who accept Jesus will be accepted by the "Son of Man" "when He comes," since the transformative deeds to be accomplished by the Son of Man are anticipated in the liberating work of Jesus.[35]

Jesus alluded in his words and deeds to the inbreaking of the reign of God. As exorcist, miracle worker, faith healer, and preacher, he demonstrated the initial signs of the presence of the Kingdom. Demonic power was being crushed through him and was being replaced by wholeness and health, characteristic signs of the presence of the reign of God. But, Ruether continues:

> The fact that one can "begin" to experience the dawning of this miracle in no way alters the fact that no Jew, including Jesus, would have spoken of the Kingdom as "already here" or the Messiah as having "already come" as long as sin continued and the evil nations maintained their sway over Israel.[36]

Regarding Jesus' preaching about the coming Son of Man, Jesus' audience would have understood the term to be synonymous with that of the Davidic Messiah. As a result, according to Ruether:

> ...the term "Son of Man" comes into prominence in the apocalypses, not when an idea of a "transcendent Son of Man" replaces the Davidic political Messiah, but rather when the role of the Davidic political Messiah comes to be more transcendentally conceived, mingling temporal and eschatological blessings. But the fact that both terms pertain primarily to the traditional role of the Messiah as King of an age of national autonomy is indicated by the fact that, when a distinction between temporal and eschatological blessings appears in later apocalyptic, the ideal of the Messiah does not split into a temporal Messiah and an eschatological "Son of Man," but rather both terms are applied to the Messiah of the temporal age, and no messianic figure at all appears in the eschatological age.[37]

Thus, the concrete political implications of messianic hope are not diluted by language about a more transcendent Messiah and Kingdom; such language only radicalizes these political hopes into a more fully cosmological transformation. While Jesus' messianic consciousness may have focused on an end to sin and sickness as signs of the inbreaking of God's Kingdom, this would not have excluded concrete political changes in the form of an expected future Davidic king to be restored along with the subjugation of Israel's imperialist enemies.[38]

Ruether insists, then, that we see Jesus as one who acted as an agent of an experience of incipient messianic blessedness for those who heeded his words and deeds. At the same time, however, she points out that this did not simplify his struggle in terms of the expectation of a Davidic Messiah (Son of Man). His religious tradition had taught him only too well that

> It is one thing to build up hope of a future Kingdom and Messiah, closely identified in intention with one's own movement. It is another to step across the divide into a proclamation that one "is" that Messiah, and that the Kingdom is here in one's own movement and revolution, when indeed the full fruits of that hope are by no means evident.[39]

Yet Jesus' ambivalence toward accepting the popular demand that he proclaim himself to be the Davidic Messiah coalesced crucially with his conviction that the Kingdom, whose advent he had been announcing, was indeed about to come. So convinced, he and his disciples went up to Jerusalem, the city where the in-breaking of the Kingdom would most assuredly occur. Thus, his riding into Jerusalem on a mule signaled to all that Jesus was clearly making some claim to the Davidic title.[40] Commenting on this, Ruether states:

> Jesus took his disciples up to Jerusalem. He expected this Reign to break in through Divine intervention and not through his own actions, and yet he was willing to use the political symbolism of that coming by entering the city in the manner of the ancient festal advent of the Davidic King and to establish himself upon the Mount of Olives from whence the final battle traditionally was to be launched by God. The denouement of these expectations was rapid, and Jesus submitted to his fate rather than to act without assurance of divine favor. His last words still ring across all the later interpretations to suggest the agony of a man uncertain as to whether the hope on which he staked his life had been in vain.[41]

Jesus' disciples, devastated by his unexpected death, witnessed the initial destruction of all their messianic hopes. How then does one account for the Easter faith that followed? Ruether states that, at best, one can find no more adequate explanation than that given by the Jewish historian, Josephus, who concluded

"Those who first loved him did not desist and up until now the race of Christians has not died out."[41]

Such inexplicable faith, which became a cry of resurrection victory, proclaimed Jesus had indeed been the Messiah, albeit in a hidden and rejected form. Certain that his resurrection vindicated their messianic hopes, Jesus' disciples were satisfied that their renewed messianic expectations would be justified. After all, he would come again—this time in glory.[43]

### Christian Interpretations of the Messiah

What must be clear at this point is that for the Jews the Messiah was a paradigmatic human being who was also a political figure, embodying all of Israel's hopes for national vindication, peace, prosperity, justice, and the defeat of its enemies. He would be an instrument of Yahweh and a symbol that the messianic age had come. The coming of the Messiah, then, and the arrival of the messianic age would happen simultaneously. Thus, evil, war, disease, oppression, and injustice of every kind would cease. This is the fundamental meaning of Hebraic messianism and its understanding of the Messiah.

The crucifixion of Jesus dashed these messianic hopes for those who believed he was the one who would be the instrument for the messianic incursion of God into history. Jesus could not be the Messiah for there was no tradition of a dying Messiah in Judaism. And, although there was a tradition of the suffering prophet, this was in no way synonymous with the Messiah.[44] Ultimately it was the disciples' experience of the crucifixion that was to generate the church's later christological response to the death of Jesus or, more specifically, it was

> ...the decision of faith made by the circle of Jesus' disciples in response to the trauma of the crucifixion. This decision of faith was a refusal to see this event as "proof" that Jesus' messianic mission had failed, and a determination to understand the crucifixion as a "necessary test" through which the messianic prophet is intended to pass in order to fulfill his salvific mission.[45]

Signs and wonders followed. Could it be that Jesus was, in fact, not dead? With the disciples' ensuing belief that, yes, "the true Prophet, Jesus" had been raised by the power of God, they began to anticipate his imminent return. God would indeed usher in the age of blessedness after all, and in so doing would vindicate the messianic mission of Jesus. "But who in Israel had ever heard of such a Messiah?"[46]

Eager to prove the messiahship of Jesus, and fueled by a belief that he had been raised from the dead, his disciples sought to confirm their faith by searching the Scriptures for possible proof. They began to interpret the psalms and prophets using a messianic midrash that became the basis for the oral New Testament.[47] This messianic midrash was nothing other than a linking together of several Old Testament texts that served as proofs that Jesus was the expected Messiah.[48] Of course, the mainstream Jewish religious community rejected this christological midrash since it violated their fundamental understanding of the meaning of the Messiah and the messianic age.

Faced with this negative response, the early Christian community included it as part of their polemic against the "unbelieving" Jews, utilizing it as a way to discredit Jewish religious leadership, their teachings and history. Christians insisted that they alone understood the real meaning of the Scriptures; it was therefore incumbent upon the hard-hearted Jews to recognize their error, repent and "accept Jesus as the true cornerstone of the covenant of salvation."[49] But

> ...this interpretation of Jesus as the cornerstone was the fundamental "stumbling block" that was to rupture the Christian from the Jewish religious community because it implied the substitution of a new foundation of the covenant for those of the tradition.[50]

Consequently, Christian preachers were excluded from teaching such an interpretation in the synogogues and ultimately this led to Christians finding themselves outside the structure of Jewish community life. Thus, "...the negative side of the christological hermeneutic began to harden in Christian preaching, changing from a prophetic appeal to the Jewish community for conversion to a fixed and final judgment upon the Jews as a rejected community."[51] This was coupled by the influx of Gentiles into the Christian community. This influx was also used as part of Christian midrash and "...one comes finally to that pattern of exegesis of the Old Testament that is characteristic of the Synoptics and the book of

Acts, where the 'rejection of the Jews' is proclaimed in tandem with the ideal of the 'election of the Gentiles.' "[52] Ruether claims Paul used this hermeneutical pattern, as well as John and the author of Hebrews, developing it into a philosophical framework that was anthropologically and cosmologically dualistic.

The church fathers both deepened and expanded the anti-Judaic christological exegesis that pre-dated and formed the hermeneutical basis of the New Testament. Patristic attitudes toward the Jews are found primarily in the *Adversus Judaeos* literature, particularly from the second to the sixth centuries. The style of this literature takes several forms but its most basic is that of a collection of Old Testament anti-Judaic and christological proof texts. They are written under several themes and fall under two major headings: (1) the rejection of the Jews and the election of the Gentiles and, (2) the inferiority of Jewish law, cult and scriptural interpretation and their spiritual fulfillment in Christianity.[53]

This interpretation is characterized by certain outstanding accusations against the Jews:

1) The Jews are rejected reprobates because they failed to accept Jesus as the Christ, an act that is the final culmination in a long history of apostasy, perfidy, and evil.

2) The Jews represent one of two peoples in the Old Testament, those who are evil and unbelieving, whereas the church is the "other people," i.e., the logical heir to a long line of faithful heroes and prophets.

3) The Gentile church inherits the election that had been promised to the Jews.

4) The reprobate status of the Jews is to last until the end of time.

5) Jewish law, cult, and scriptural interpretation are characterized by carnality, legalism, and literalism vis-a-vis Christianity, which is superior ontologically, morally, and historically.[54]

*Theological Consequences*
Ruether asserts that there are several fundamental theological structures that perpetuate the Christian anti-Judaic myth. Rethinking these structures is essential if Jewish-Christian relations are to improve in any significant way. She is aware of the risks involved in this undertaking but believes they must be faced, not only to insure improved relations with the Jewish community, but

also for a less spurious Christian identity. She cites three basic theological dualisms that she claims have been the basis for the earliest Christian self-understanding and simultaneously for the negation of Judaism.

1) One of these dualisms she calls the schism of judgment and promise. This was the exegetical basis of Christian theology before the New Testament was written and it was later incorporated into its theology and exegesis. It was basically a Christian midrash on the psalms and prophets that, on the one hand, sought to prove that the Hebrew Scriptures predicted Jesus as the Messiah and, on the other hand, demonstrated the apostasy and perfidy of the Jews in their refusal to accept Jesus as such. This hermeneutical method was more fully adopted by the church fathers who continued this tradition of proof-texting to build both christological and anti-Judaic arguments.[55]

The fundamental flaw in this type of exegesis, according to Ruether, is that it distorted the prophetic dialectic of judgment and promise. Its positive side of forgiveness and promise was applied to the church, while its negative side of wrath and judgment was directed against the Jews. Prophetic criticism is primarily self-criticism. The church, by failing to apply the negative side of the dialectic to itself, made self-criticism impossible. Consequently, it opened itself to ecclesiastical triumphalism and an infallibility complex.[56]

Christian scholars of the "Old Testament" no longer interpret the Scriptures this way, but the problem is not so easily solved in the New Testament. Anti-Judaic exegesis is expressed in the New Testament by interpreting Jesus' denunciations of hypocritical religion as a rejection of Judaism. This manner of interpretation is used to deny the value of the Law in its entirety.[57]

Ruether suggests two ways to correct such schismatic reading of the Scriptures: the first is the recognition of the true meaning of prophetic religion as *internal* self-criticism and to apply it to Christian faith as such. The second is for Christian theologians to purge themselves of any anti-Judaic biases in the way they interpret the gospel and do theology. This means being able to affirm Judaism, its rabbinic tradition, and Jesus' role within that context.[58]

2) Another dualism that Ruether claims has promoted anti-Judaism is the schism of particularism and universalism. A truly universal or catholic faith does not impose its specific cultural/

historical experience of the divine upon others, implying that its religious experience is superior to others and the only source of truth. Such an attitude is imperialistic and, according to Ruether, "is the absolutization of one particularism."[59] Judaism can teach Christians much here, for Jews have not, in Ruether's estimation, adopted this attitude. Rather, they have recognized the right of all people to define their own self-understanding and relationship to God according to their own religious culture.[60] To correct this schism Christians must come to realize that

> ...this unity of God as Creator and Redeemer cannot be said to be incarnated in one people and their historical revelation, giving them the right to conquer and absorb all the others. The only universality which can be truly said to be "of God" is one that transcends every particularity, guaranteeing the integrity of each people to stand before God in their own identities and histories (Mic. 4, 5).[61]

This attitude can correct the false universalism that is really masked imperialism. It accepts instead a limited particularism that respects other religious cultures, affirming by this that "only God is one and universal."[62]

3) Using dualisms adopted from apocalyptic Judaism and Greek philosophy, Christian theology perpetuated a third anti-Judaic dualism that Ruether brings together under the schisms of law and grace, letter and spirit, old and new Adam. Jews became identified with the "old" law of Moses, with legalism, and with an inferior covenant, whereas Christians saw themselves on a superior spiritual plane because they represented grace, spirit, and the new Adam in Christ.[63] As a result,

> The Jews were relegated both to a past and to a morally and ontologically inferior status of existence as their ongoing identity from the time of Jesus to the end of history (which was then projected back on their identity in Old Testament times as well). Christianity transcends Judaism historically, morally, and ultimately. It is the fulfillment of that which Judaism merely "foreshadowed" in the "fleshly way."[64]

Realized eschatology and fulfilled messianism became the twin horns of this dilemma that converted the dialectics of biblical faith into anti-Judaic dualisms. Upon this the structure of classical christology has been erected.

Ruether insists that the anti-Judaic dualisms she has named are, in fact, essential components of early christological thought. As a result, Christian understandings of Jesus as the Christ are often predicated on a virulent form of religious imperialism, whose base has been structured around claims of fulfilled messianism and realized eschatology.

In such imperialism, fulfilled messianism means that the Messiah has come in Jesus, that in him the promises of salvation have been fulfilled. Consequently, since the Jews have rejected Jesus as the Messiah, they have lost their status as the elect of Yahweh and revealed themselves to be a perfidious and apostate people, whose teachers are spiritually blind and whose exegesis is fundamentally erroneous.

Furthermore, given this rejection of Jesus by the Jews, the Christian church has become the new elect of Yahweh, the embodiment of the messianic promises, the sole receptor of true faith and the only valid witness to the revelation and experience of God. Thus, "to be saved all must incorporate themselves into the one true human identity, the Christian faith."[65]

As Christianity grew in power and authority, "fulfilled messianism then became the new foundation for the ideological universalism of the Christian Roman Empire."[66] Historically this has resulted in an imperialistic perspective that has denied all other religious bodies any partial claim to truth, and any right to authentic existence. Thus, Christianity's particular and limited religious experience took on a universalism that has been the basis of an oppressive Christian missiology for centuries.[67]

At the same time, the anti-Judaic dualisms found in Christian theological patterns have led to what Ruether calls the "historicizing and spiritualizing of the eschatological." This means that the church reinterpreted Christ's coming, not as one of several events originally understood as ecstatic signs of the nearness of the Kingdom, but rather as a new phase in salvation history. More specifically, the church interpreted the originally Jewish symbols of Messiah, resurrection, coming of the Holy Spirit, and New Covenant, not as signs of the approaching Kingdom, but rather as events that signaled a new religious institution, a new historical era and a new elect of God whose existence superseded that of Israel. It did this by interpreting these symbols outside of their original prophetic context. Ruether challenges Christianity to recognize this and to understand these symbols *eschatologically,* that is, "...as realities toward which we are still moving," not as *historical* events that became bases for the establishment of the Christian church. In addition, by "spiritualizing the eschatological" (a later explanation found in Paul and John) Christianity converted the concept of the Kingdom into a spiritual or interior matter, a reality found in the heart of the individual. This has also led to an individualistic, privatized and ahistorical understanding of the Kingdom.[68] What both of these perspectives did was to insist that belief in Jesus as the Christ and in the Christian church as the instrument of Christ in the world was the only way to God. Ultimately, Ruether maintains these perspectives led to anti-Semitism in particular and a general spirit of condescension in relation to other faith traditions.

In searching for a common eschatological meeting ground between Judaism and Christianity, Ruether suggests Christians recognize that the fullness of the Christ event, by its very nature, cannot be divorced from the coming of the Kingdom. Rather, both must be seen as an event which ever remains in the future, both transcendentally and eschatologically. Such a vision will admit to historical moments in which the transcendent becomes present in an anticipatory way, (moments of profound repentance, reconciliation, justice, liberation, etc.,), but those moments are never to be more than relative, never absolutized. This is because the eschatological is always ahead of us, drawing us on beyond past accomplishments to deeper insights and greater truth.[69]

> Such an understanding of the eschatological as the principle of self-transcendence in history, as a power which can become proleptically present and fruitful of creative work but is never wholly immanentized in such work, that remains essentially ahead of us, always available for new self-transcendence—such a view may be a key for solving the theological dilemma that stands between Christianity and Judaism. If the key is to work Christianity will have to recognize its own experience of Jesus not as the absolute coming of Christ but rather as a relative instance of the drawing near of the eschatological. Indeed, is not this

view already suggested in the Christian doctrine that we still look forward to the "final" coming?[70]

Ruether offers this view as a possible solution both Christians and Jews might embrace as a way to understand the eschatological, one that precludes the need to invalidate each other's authentic religious experiences.

It has been argued throughout this chapter that for the Jewish people, the coming of the Messiah and the coming of the messianic Kingdom are identical. Further, Ruether has pointed out time and again that messianic hope for Israel was not bound up in the coming of a salvific person, but was, more correctly, an anticipation of that time in history when evil would no longer have sway, when the lion would lie down with the lamb, when peace would rule the nations, when every unjust social structure would be dismantled. In her own words:

> ...if there is anything the reign of God was supposed to be about, it was about a change that was so public and obvious that it didn't need to be argued about. That any such change, even in the sense of "progress" (moral progress, that is), has indeed separated Christian times or world history from the time of Jesus until now is not very convincing to many people.[71]

In "Messiah of Israel," Ruether argues that this cosmological christology both "evacuated the historical person of Jesus," and simultaneously insisted that what it claimed could literally be traced to the historical Jesus. She further argues that the christology of Chalcedon—which defined Jesus not as a human *person*, but rather as a being possessing only a human nature that was united with the "person" and the "nature" of the Logos—was a distortion.

For Ruether, this interpretation, whereby the *historical* "person" of Jesus was replaced by the *cosmological* "person" of the Logos, meant that "the historical person of Jesus was replaced by an archetypal symbol of ideal humanity." In her estimation, therefore, orthodox christology in its mature form replaced the historical person of Jesus with a cosmological myth that issued from contemporary religious philosophy. In this assessment, Jesus becomes the historical catalyst that occasioned the myth "of the sacramental appearance, in the 'representative Man,' of essential [humankind] and creation," not as they are, but rather as they should be. In this sense, christology is less about Jesus than it is about making Jesus the symbol of all that humankind and creation should be. In the final analysis then, Ruether sees classical christology as "...the myth of transcendent or ideal anthropology and cosmology."[72]

But Israel was not willing to accept a cosmological myth as the basis for its messianic hope, particularly because the Kingdom had not come. Hence, Ruether argues that such a refusal reflected "an authentic judgment based upon their own historical experience of such messianic proclamations...."[73] By this statement she demonstrates that she is both sympathetic to the integrity of the Jewish position and critical of the anti-Judaic, Christian polemic that reinterpreted Hebrew messianism for the primary purpose of Christian self-legitimation. Thus she concludes that, for her, "Jesus is not yet the Christ."[74] In a very qualified way she offers this alternative:

> If Jesus is to serve as our paradigm of [the human], then he must not be seen simply as a finalization of an ideal, but one who reveals to us the structure of human existence as it stands in that point of tension between what is and what ought to be. We might say that Jesus is our paradigm of hoping, aspiring [humanity], venturing his life in expectation of the Kingdom, and Christ stands as the symbol of the fulfillment of that hope. Jesus Christ, then, stands for that unification of [humankind] with [its] destiny which has still not come, but in whose light we continue to hope and struggle.[75]

Here is no closed model of christology, but one that offers the possibility for renewal according to the needs of every historical age.

## Two Suggested Corrections

For Ruether, then, who has been deeply influenced by her study of the development of christology in Judaism and early Christianity, the statement "Jesus is the Christ" makes sense only insofar as it is an affirmation that is "paradigmatic for the structure of human existence and not something unique about Jesus."[76] In other words, to say "Jesus is the Christ" can only mean, for her, that Jesus is a paradigmatic person who represents all human beings who aspire to make God's will done on this earth as it is in heaven, and who, being so stretched by their hope that the Kingdom will come, radically alter in concrete ways the power of evil in this world.

When Ruether says, therefore, that "Jesus is the Christ," she is making a claim about the ongoing possibilities inherent in being human. Among these possibilities are an increase in the human capacity for conversion, mutuality, courage, peace, love, justice, and compassion that we as women and men are challenged by Jesus to embody on this earth. To respond to such a possibility is to diminish the tension between what is and what ought to be, thereby contributing to a more just and human world order. For Ruether, this authentic living of one's humanity will require the same price of Christians today as it did of Jesus, namely, the cross. As she sees it, Christians and Jews are in a similar historical situation, though they journey by different routes, because both are struggling to make the Kingdom come on this earth by being faithful to their own religious heritages.

Ruether has proposed what she considers to be two fundamental steps necessary to correct the anti-Judaic and imperialistic patterns of christology. First, Christian faith in Jesus as the Christ must be expressed in terms that are proleptic and anticipatory, not final and fulfilled. Christians must not claim that Jesus fulfilled Jewish messianic hopes because, in fact, he did not. Instead, Christians must begin to see Jesus as one who both announced and embodied messianic hope in his words and deeds, but who did so without the earthly satisfaction of that hope being fulfilled. As Christians, we continue to proclaim and experience that hope in his name amid the dialectics of human existence. But the Kingdom still eludes us. Our power to persevere in the struggle issues from our memory of Jesus' resurrection, which enables us to continue to hope the Kingdom will come and to believe evil will not have the last word.[77]

Second, Ruether suggests that christology be understood paradigmatically as well as proleptically. It must be understood as relative to a particular people with a particular history and religious experience. Christians cannot claim that belief in Jesus is the only way, or a superior way, to God. As she has said, "He may indeed be the only name *for us*. But other names continue to be named and do not fail to bear fruit."[78] She suggests that we cease to use

Jesus' name to deny the validity of other people's religious experiences. Such a stance can unite not only Christians and Jews but Christians and adherents of other world religions as well. The result can be a vital bond of solidarity which, while recognizing differences, can nonetheless be a way to mediate hope in the face of anguish and defeat, a hope that is determined to make the Kingdom come in a more visible way on this earth.[79]

## Questions for Reflection and Discussion

1. What is the origin of Jewish messianism? Explain the idea of the Messiah found within this tradition.

2. What was the contribution of the eighth century prophets to the understanding of Hebraic messianism?

3. How did the earliest disciples seek to prove Jesus was the Messiah and what was their response to other Jews who refused to accept him as such?

4. According to Ruether, what was the contribution of the church fathers to Christian anti-Judaism?

5. Discuss the three theological dualisms that, according to Ruether, formed the basis for the Christian negation of Judaism.

6. Ruether is critical of the "cosmological Christology" of Chalcedon and offers an alternative understanding of "Jesus-as-the-Christ." Explain both her criticism and her alternative view. What is your response to each?

7. Discuss the two basic changes Ruether insists must take place to correct the anti-Judaic and imperialistic patterns of Christology. Do you agree or disagree?

# ☙ CHAPTER 3

# The Christology of Rosemary Radford Ruether: Liberation Theology, Ecology, Women, and the Christological Tradition

## Liberation Theology

Ruether's study of the idea of the Messiah/Christ in early Judaism and Christianity is responsible for her ensuing critique of the anti-Judaism she discovered in traditional christological formulations. At the same time, this study provides her with an understanding of the historical Jesus, one who linked the biblical prophetic-messianic vision with his mission to proclaim the Kingdom. As a result, she has written:

> The cutting edge of the prophetic word operates as a gift of discernment. Hence it cannot be translated into a dogma or fixed formula. The appropriate word has to be discovered in new ways in new situations. I believe that this is exactly the process that we see going on in the biblical prophets and also in Jesus' use of the message of the King-

dom. Jesus' announcement of the Kingdom is not Zealot revenge politics, but neither is it a neutralizing transcendentalism, as so many Christian commentators would have it. It strikes at the heart of the political corruption, but in a way that brings it home to his own society rather than just projecting it against the enemies of Israel. It is in Latin American liberation theology that I think we are discovering a new starting point for linking biblical messianic hope with the mission of Jesus.[1]

In sympathy with the Jews over the Christian distortion of the Jewish idea of the Messiah, Ruether is likewise in sympathy with Third World liberation theologians' efforts to recover the historical Jesus and "the political dimension of biblical messianic faith."[2] Both efforts confirm, in many respects, her own christological vision as it has developed over the years.[3]

*Recovering the Historical Jesus*
In conjunction with Third World liberation theologians, Ruether affirms that the starting point for christology is the historical Jesus, particularly his praxis: his efforts to transform the world in which he lived. This is the key to understanding his person and message. Liberation theologians claim that the most basic characteristic of Jesus' actions is that they reveal his preferential option for the poor and oppressed. Thus, "the following of Christ must start with this critical option for the poor."[4]

Using Isaiah 61 and Luke 4, Ruether has pointed out how liberation theologians have concluded that the poor and oppressed are God's primary concern, evidenced in Jesus' deeds of preaching the good news to the poor, setting captives free, giving sight to the blind, etc. They have also concluded that Jesus' actions on behalf of the most vulnerable are also a critical judgment upon the rich and powerful. God's option for the poor and oppressed demands that the wrong done to them by the social and religious elites be vindicated. It is they who will enter the Kingdom of God ahead of those who oppressed them on this earth. The only hope of salvation the rich and powerful have is to renounce the wealth and power they have accrued at the expense of the poor and join Jesus in his solidarity with the dispossessed.[5]

Ruether believes Jesus' vision of the Kingdom was "this-wordly, social and political,"[6] rather than eschatological. She bases this belief on the parables and historical sayings attributed to Jesus, especially the Lord's prayer. Using this prayer, she argues that the Kingdom means that God's will shall be done on earth, that basic human needs shall be fulfilled on physical, social, and spiritual levels. For her, the coming of the Kingdom also means that human evil will be overcome and that, insofar as it is possible, circumstances conducive to right relationship with God and with one another will be established on earth.[7]

Ruether likewise insists that Jesus' vision of the Kingdom was grounded in a radical realization of the deep roots of oppression. She believes he saw these roots as a fundamental desire for power, prestige, and wealth that culminated in a lust for domination over others. It was this alienating lust for domination that Jesus sought to expose and to replace with his own example of loving service. She also points out that Jesus' message, praxis and vision of the Kingdom was not primarily a spiritual matter:

> The fundamental sins of lust for power, prestige and wealth express themselves fundamentally in social oppression. Jesus' critique of social oppression is directed primarily against the elites of his own community. These include the political elites, Herod and his family; the land-holding nobility, who reduce peasants to indentured servants; and the religious elites, who use the temple and the Law to lord it over the unwashed, uneducated and outcast.[8]

This critique is good news to the poor and oppressed because its aim is to overturn all unjust social structures kept intact by the privileges enjoyed as a result of wealth, rank, education and religious observance. Thus "Jesus' vision of the Kingdom is one of radical social iconoclasm."[9] He sought to undo all those unjust structures that keep people in oppressive relationships by offering an alternative vision of mutuality, peace, and justice for all.

Ruether's understanding of Jesus' vision of the Kingdom is consonant with that proposed by Central and Latin American liberation theologians. For them, too, the coming of the Kingdom is experienced in *this* world, wherever poverty, disease, injustice, and oppression are overcome.[10] However, in explaining liberation theology's vision of the Kingdom, Ruether is very careful to say that it does not expect any social system to completely embody the

Kingdom since it recognizes that every social system is limited and inadequate.

> Yet this does not reduce all social systems and situations to the same level. There are some situations which are closer to the Kingdom than others, not in an evolutionary progressive way, but in the sense of signs and meditations of the Kingdom which better disclose what God's intention is for humankind.... Some situations disclose greater justice and mutuality; some systems allow for greater justice and mutuality.[11]

Ruether, like many Latin American liberation theologians, asserts that the temporal task of those claiming to be Christian is to participate in concretizing Jesus' vision of the Kingdom. That is to say, to denounce everything in human society that creates oppression and alienation and to promote all that makes humankind a community characterized by mutuality, freedom, justice, and peace.[12]

*Implications for Christology*
What does Ruether see as the implications for a Christology written from a liberationist perspective? Such a perspective means: (1) starting with the historical Jesus; (2) claiming that his actions, the key to his message and person, reveal his preferential option for the poor and oppressed; and (3) restoring to the center of Christianity the particular understanding of the Kingdom of God as an earth-oriented society of peace, justice, and mutuality.

Ruether would argue that these implications negate any idea of fulfilled messianism. First, liberationist christology, in its effort to restore the historical Jesus to the center of Christian self-understanding, heralds "the unfinished mandate of messianic hope."[13] This means it recognizes that our hope is for a salvation that begins in this world, socially and historically. Likewise, it means continuing to expose the chasm between what is and what ought to be, while participating in the struggle to eliminate the injustices responsible for the chasm. Finally, it means seeing Jesus as the messianic prophet who embodied this hope in an exemplary way, rather than spiritualizing our understanding of him so that "...the Christ-nature is realized inwardly without having to deal with the contradictions of an unregenerate world."[14]

Second, in Ruether's interpretation, a liberationist christology means an end to the "language of finality" the church has used about Jesus.[15] Jesus did not fulfill Jewish messianic hopes, nor did he establish the reign of God in any final way on this earth. Neither did he overcome all evil or deliver us from it unquestionably. The language of finality obscures historical reality and is a betrayal of the historical Jesus who confronted the realities of suffering, sin, and death concretely in his lifetime, rather than instructing people to endure suffering passively in lieu of a better, other-worldly life to come.[16]

Third, a liberationist christology implies that the church must reject any ideological christology that justifies an oppressive status quo for the benefit of a few. It must repudiate every attempt to claim Christ as the source or vindicator of any dominant social hierarchy or system that is racist, classist, or imperialistic.[17]

Fourth, a liberationist christology implies that the church, like Jesus, will make a preferential option for the poor and oppressed. Thus, the church must be willing to forego its privileged place in society and to endure the lot of the most vulnerable, i.e. it must be willing to undergo persecution, torture, and death. "For to follow Christ's preferential option for the poor in Latin America means to be ready to follow him into the grave."[18]

Fifth, a liberationist christology means taking a profoundly new look at the meaning of redemptive suffering in light of the reign of evil and death that characterize Central and Latin America. It is a rejection of any interpretation of the cross of Christ that promotes passivity or neurotic guilt in the face of suffering. For liberation theology the God of Jesus did not seek or desire Jesus' suffering any more than God desires the suffering of any human being. Consequently, a liberationist christology implies naming poverty, suffering and death as evils to be overcome, not afflictions from God to be endured in a spirit of filial obedience. From the perspective of a liberationist christology, the only response to the death of Jesus, and to those who continue to die today as unjustly as he did, is for the living to carry on the struggle against the principalities and powers responsible for such deaths.[19]

> Indeed their very death becomes a rallying point for new energy. In their name people now organize themselves to renew the work of liberation. The memory of their lives becomes stronger than the powers of death and gives peo-

ple hope that the powers of death can be broken. This is the real meaning of redemptive suffering, of Jesus and of Christians, not passive or masochistic self-sacrifice.[20]

Liberationist christology is overtly political and has made it impossible for anyone to claim neutrality in their understanding of Jesus as the Christ. That is to say, liberationist christology has exposed how oppressive the classic images of Christ in Latin America have been for the majority of people there.[21] Given this, to claim neutrality is to ignore the fact that those very images of Christ have blatantly maintained the injustices of the status quo. Liberation theology also has exposed how closely aligned with politics traditional christology has been, particularly whenever it has been utilized by ecclesiastical and social elites to secure power and privileges. This theology has revealed how some traditional christologies have and continue to operate within a network of oppressive socio-political structures. Understandably, then, a liberationist christological perspective has several socio-political implications.

First, drawing from Ruether, this christological proposal demands an unequivocal identification with the poor and oppressed after the examples of Jesus. This calls for participation in the ongoing struggle against injustice. In some concrete ways, then, one's christology must necessarily influence one's political affiliation, for the litmus test of a political position would be how close its agenda comes to prioritizing the needs of the poor over the wants of the comfortable and wealthy.

Second, Ruether indicates how such an understanding of Jesus implies a willingness to recognize the vast interstructuring of injustices—sexism, racism, classism, and imperialism—and the role dominant ideologies play in keeping the injustices intact. Thus it demands a willingness to allow oneself to be "stretched" intellectually, spiritually, emotionally, and politically, in order to be able to perceive that "the system" maintains itself by pitting men against women, whites against people of color, poor and working class against one another and against the middle class, and Western neo-colonialism against indigenous struggles for a socialist alternative.

Third, on a socio-political level, Ruether shows that a liberationist christology which claims that Jesus espoused a preferential option for the poor demands a candid recognition of the limits of capitalism. Despite the language of mystification that extols the virtues of this system, capitalism has wrought widespread economical social, political and spiritual inequities. Any serious consideration of christology from a liberationist perspective implies a recognition of the potential value of an indigenous socialism, not only in Central and Latin America, but in the United States as well.[22]

By claiming that the historical Jesus embodied a preferential option for the poor and oppressed, and that the coming of the Kingdom begins concretely on this earth, liberationist christology has thereby revealed the apostasy of every individualistic, privatized, other-worldly, and spiritualized understanding of Jesus. It has also shown that such understandings of Jesus have made him malleable in the hands of an imperialistic, sexist, racist, and classist church and society. To appropriate a liberationist christology, therefore, is to actively side with the poor, oppressed, and marginalized of this world. The implications of such a posture reach deeply into every level of our lives: personal, religious, economic, social, and political. This, no doubt, has been reason enough for the principalities and powers in both church and society to make every effort to discredit such a perspective.

Ruether insists that "the messianic mandate is not a finished 'deposit of faith' of the past. It is a revelation of our authentic future, the risen future of Christ, which is still ahead of us."[23]

## Ecology and Christology

Rosemary Radford Ruether also has been concerned about ecology and its connection to christology. In fact, she is among the first theologians to make this connection.[24] It is central to her hope for a "new humanity" and a "new earth," a hope rooted in her understanding of the messianic vision of Jesus.

*The Original Vision*
According to Ruether, in Hebraic thought there is one covenant of creation, which includes a harmonious relationship between nature and society. Breaking this covenant means establishing social injustice and cultivating natural calamities. "This Hebrew prophetic sense of the interconnection of harmony with nature and social justice is particularly important for the construction of an ethic of eco-justice."[25]

The covenant of creation is clearly expressed in the vision of redemption found in the prophetic-messianic tradition. In the Hebrew Scriptures this tradition offered a vision of a new age of peace, justice, and harmony that was expected to occur in history. The Hebrew idea of the Jubilee was one redemptive paradigm that embodied this vision. As Ruether explains it:

> The Jubilee teaches that there are certain basic elements that make for life as God intended it on earth. Everyone has their own vine and fig tree. No one is enslaved to another. The land and animals are not overworked. But human sinfulness tends to create a drift away from this intended state. Some people's land is expropriated by others. People are sold into bondage. Nature is overworked. So, on a periodic basis, there must be a revolutionary conversion. Unjust debts...must be liquidated. Those who are sold into slavery are released; the land that has been expropriated is returned. Land and animals are allowed to rest. Humanity and nature recover their just balance.[26]

Several passages from Isaiah also embody this messianic vision of redemption. According to Ruether, Jesus announced this vision when he began his public ministry. In doing so, he proclaimed the prophetic-messianic vision of the Kingdom as a time in history when the will of God would be done on earth, when basic human needs would be met, and when temptation and evil would be avoided.[27] The implications include a hoped-for time when domination of every kind would cease and when all people would live in right relationship with God, one another, and the created world.

## Distortions and Aberrations

Ruether sees in the history of Christianity the development of a false consciousness that distorts Jesus' vision of redemption. It is a consciousness of reality that is based on a hierarchical system of domination and alienation which denies the relationship between humankind and nature, leaving nature to be used and abused by men. Like women and other oppressed groups, nature is perceived to be under male domination and control.[28]

Commenting on Ruether's discussion of this, Judith Vaughan writes that in Western Christianity this dualism became a part of a religious worldview that included the separation of "spiritual men" from the natural world. This dualism has been translated into religious language by opposing nature and grace, earth and heaven, world and church, historical and transcendent. These dualisms, which are rooted in both classical neo-Platonism and apocalyptic Judaism, represent a shift "...from the original Hebrew messianic hope which was futuristic but this-worldly."[29]

Given these aberrations, Ruether argues that two basic models of creation of nature have shaped the Western Christian imagination. The first understands nature as a hierarchy or "great chain of being." The second sees nature as continually developing toward historical maturity and perfection. In some ways this second model parallels the messianic vision; however, according to Ruether, both models have become representations of an ideology of social bigotry.[30]

In the first model, God as "pure Spirit" crowns the chain of being. Angels, humankind, animals, plants, and rocks follow in that order. Each level is ontologically and morally superior to the level below and thus rules it accordingly. God rules all, the angels rule the universe, and humans rule creation. This hierarchy is translated in the human community to mean that men rule over women, masters over slaves, and whites over people of color. Just as God rules the whole created order, the head rules the body and "men" rule the created order "below them." "Thus the great chain of being mandates both the social hierarchy of ruling-class males over others and the hierarchy of man over nature (exercised, in practice, by ruling-class males)."[31]

The second model, progressivism, is understood as an evolutionary or revolutionary model of history. It presupposes that a process of infinite expansion within history can result in a period of final perfection. Ruether maintains that this perspective contains several contradictions and also assumes that particular groups of people are the preferred agents of historical progress. In the lead are white, Anglo-Saxon, Protestant males. The "others" are barely considered in this march toward unlimited development. Applied in reverse, the progressive eon reaches its culmination with the "others" defeating their oppressors and thereby inheriting the earth. Thus, the messianic vision, which inspires this second model, is reduced to a "theology of revenge."[32]

*Conversion: An Alternative Model*

As a feminist theologian, Ruether questions both of these models of nature and the humankind-nature relationship they advocate. She suggests an alternative model of "conversion" as a way to develop a just and balanced society that encourages harmonious relationships with the environment."[33]

With this in mind, she urges us to build relations with nature and each other that are based on mutuality and service. She has pointed to Jesus' vision of messianic hope as the beacon to guide us in these right relationships. Ruether's understanding of the Lordship of Christ as servanthood can be applied to the way Christians relate to nature. Further, Jesus' example of servanthood is an example of the end of hierarchy in all relationships, including the humankind/nature relation.

> We must learn to use the gift of intelligence as servant rather than master of nature, to refine and sustain those processes by which nature renews itself, renews its own life processes, and generates an infinite variety of creatures. Only by making human intelligence the expression of a "good gardener," rather than a destroyer and exploiter, can we learn to live in harmony with nature as a friend on the earth, helping to sustain and enhance those processes of life renewal for the sake both of our progeny and of all earth's creatures.[34]

Only then can Jesus' example of servanthood point us in the direction of the "shalom of God" where the prophetic messianic vision of redemptive hope is renewed again and again in every effort to promote peace, justice, and harmony on earth.

# Women and Christology

Ruether has stated that "christology has been the doctrine of the Christian tradition that has been most frequently used against women."[35] Certainly one reason for this is Christianity's misinterpretation of the Messiah and the messianic age, a misinterpretation that culminated by the fifth century in the development of an imperialistic, hierarchical, cosmological, and patriarchal christology.[36] In light of this, the following section discusses certain historical developments that have fostered a christology that dehumanizes rather than liberates.

*Key Historical Developments*

When Jesus did not return in glory as the early Christians expected, they reinterpreted his role. He became the mediator linking heaven and earth and they attributed to him such titles as Savior, Mosaic Prophet, Revealer, and Messenger. Thus, roles originally associated with "Messiah"—such as apocalyptic warrior, eschatological judge, raiser of the dead, King of the Age to Come—were separated from Jesus' historical life and posited in the future. They were not seen as anticipations of the messianic age beginning in his life and death. Yet it was firmly believed he would come again and exercise these messianic roles.[37]

> So the paradox of Christian Christology *vis a vis* its Jewish background is that the prime title for Jesus continued to be Christ (Messiah), yet his actual historical role came to be seen in terms of functions which were pre- or nonmessianic. The Jewish title "Messiah," therefore, differs from the Christian title "Christ" precisely because the paradox of an "already experienced messianic event" created a problem whereby the title "Christ" must needs be expanded to cover a host of roles within history which were not originally associated with the Messiah, and the primary meaning of Messiah as "King of the Age to Come" faded from the center of attention.[38]

In "Messiah of Israel" Ruether states that each of these historical mediating roles and the final eschatological roles were absorbed into a cosmological doctrine. In turn, Jesus came to be understood as both Revealer and Messiah because he was both the primordial principle whereby God's self-manifestation became known to humankind and also the means by which the world was crated. Thus, "eschatology was refounded upon transcendent cosmology."[39] Such a strategy made it possible for the church fathers to appropriate th eschatological myth of the Messiah by utilizing classical philosophy, culture, and society and, in particular, by using the cosmogonic myth of a divine Logos "as the Key."[40]

Ruether has stated that in Logos christology Christ is seen both as the liberating Messiah who stands over against worldly power and domination, and as the original Logos-Wisdom of God through which the world is created, guided, ruled, and reconciled to God.[41]

This linking of the messianic idea of new being with the original foundations of creation was necessary to prevent Christian theology from splitting into a dualism between redemption and creation, the dualistic pattern into which gnosticism had fallen. Cosmological Christology saved mainstream Christianity from this dualism between creation and redemption. By saying that the liberating Messiah is also the Logos through which the world was created, Christianity could say that our new liberated being does not contradict our created being but rather vindicates and fulfills its true nature and potential.[42]

Ruether, however, insists there were two ways of looking at this relationship:

If *both* the original and the true being of things are set over against the oppressive powers of the world, then Christ continues to be a symbol of our authentic selves over against systems of injustice. Resistance to injustice has an even firmer foundation. But if the Logos is seen as the foundation of the powers of the world, then Christology becomes integrated back into a world view that sacralizes the existing systems of sexism, slavery and imperialism and sees these as the "order of creation."[43]

According to Ruether, in the second and third centuries Christianity was a religion in conflict with the state of Rome and therefore embodied the first liberating Logos view. But, when Christianity became part and parcel of Roman society, particularly under the Edict of Constantine, it embraced the second dominating Logos view. Thus the lordship of Christ no longer liberated the most vulnerable in that society, specifically, women, slaves, and conquered people. Instead it became a platform of power and domination for those who, deriving their lordship from the lordship of Christ, used their privileged positions to subjugate those under their jurisdiction.[44]

Further, Ruether states that "the term Logos as the divine identity for Christ should have been a term that pointed all humans to the foundations of their true humanity."[45] However, because the Greek and Hellenist Jewish tradition took shape in a patriarchal culture, the terms Logos and Christ developed with an androcentric bias. This happened, according to her, because rationality was presumed to be normatively male in patriarchal culture. As a result, all theological references for defining Christ were androcentrically biased. Essential humanity, the image of God in humanity, along with the Logos of God, were interrelated in these androcentric definitions. Ultimately they reinforced the presupposition that God was male and that Christ, who reveals the male God, must likewise be male.[46]

Ruether traces the development of Logos christology showing how it reflected Greek political thought of the time and supported a view of the emperor as one who represented the *nous* or mind of God which governed the universe.[47] This view reached zenith proportions in Eusebius of Caesarea, the court theologian of the Emperor Constantine whose famous edict in C.E. 313 legitimized Christianity and made it the religion of the empire. The christological consequences of this intimate church-state relationship were far-reaching. They came on the heels of a growing movement away from an initially charismatic and apocalyptic christology where both male and female prophets spoke in the spirit of Jesus. This was replaced by an institutionalized ministry of bishops who monopolized the right to interpret and speak of Jesus' name and who designated themselves (males) as the only legitimate representatives of apostolic authority.[48] Thus, by the time of Eusebius, christology was already developing in directions that were patriarchal, hierarchical, and imperialistic.

In such a context, Constantine was regarded as the earthly Vicar of Christ and promoted as such by Eusebius. With Christianity established as the official religion of the empire, it was believed that the Kingdom of the Christ had come. And so:

> The cosmic theology, which regarded Jesus as the incarnation of the Cosmic Logos, could be used to integrate the political realm with the cosmic realm, regarding Constantine as representing the same providential role in the political cosmos that Christ represents in the natural and metaphysical cosmos. All the messianic hope for the coming of a King "after God's own heart," who would establish God's reign over the earth, could be translated into a new ideological sanctification of the new Christian empire. Therefore all the hopes for messianic blessedness could be inte-

grated with the new Christian imperial order to bless it in the name of those very hopes by which Christians had formerly opposed the pagan Roman Empire.[49]

Both Constantine and Eusebius sought to give witness to the establishment of Christ's reign on earth. This ideological alignment of Constantine with Christ and the empire with Christendom sanctified the existing structures of patriarchy, hierarchy, slavery, and Greco-Roman imperialism. Christ as the Logos, God's mediator who governs the world, was identified with Constantine, who in fact governed the empire. A vast hierarchy of being operated wherein women, slaves, and non-Christians were ruled and defined by their superiors who were understood to be *the* representatives of the Logos. Christology became a tool of oppression against the most lowly or "other," the least of whom were women. Labeled inferior to men in the order of creation, women were therefore unable to represent Christ ontologically, morally, or intellectually.[50]

Women suffered greatly and uniquely from these developments, particularly because they affected the Christian interpretation of the *imago dei*. As Ruether maintains:

> ...practically the whole patristic and medieval tradition rejected the possibility that women were equally theomorphic....Most of the Church fathers concluded that it was the male who possessed the image of God normatively, whereas women in themselves did not possess the image of God, but rather were the image of the body or the lower creation, which man was given to rule over.[51]

This is evidenced, for example, in the theology of Augustine where the influence of Greek philosophy is apparent. Augustine's theology took the form of a male-female dualism whose provenance is found in the Platonic soul-body dualism. In this dualistic anthropology the soul was considered the higher, spiritual, intellectual principle, but the body was the lower, carnal, material principle. Although Augustine believed Adam was whole in his person, he also believed he was composed of a double nature, i.e., male spirit and female bodiliness. Eve represented the "lower" bodily side of Adam when she was taken from him. Her task was to be his helpmate, primarily in procreation, for as Augustine taught, a male is always more suitable for any spiritual task. Because he believed a woman's body or carnal nature was inferior to that of a man's spiritual nature, he considered woman to be lower in the order of creation and more prone to sin. As a result, Augustine taught that the male alone possessed the full image of God; the female could only image God fully in conjunction with a male. Consequently, woman was not considered to be a whole person who images God in her own right. Such a definition of woman has resulted in her being understood as naturally subordinate and inferior to man, incapable of fully imaging God except through man.[52]

This negative view of woman as found in Augustine and other church fathers was amplified in the later scholastic theology of Thomas Aquinas. Indeed, Ruether claims, it was he who most clearly formulated a sexist christological perspective. Thomas, who believed women were "misbegotten males," was deeply influenced by Aristotelian biology, according to which the male sperm contained the genetic form of the embryo, while the woman's contribution was merely to provide the matter that would give flesh to the embryonic form. When the female matter caused any deformation of the male seed, it produced a defective human being, i.e., a woman. Consequently, Thomas held that the male was the normative representative of humanity. Woman, born as the result of a biological accident, coupled with her bodily, carnal nature, was defective ontologically, morally, and intellectually. Thus, she was to be subject to man in the social order. From this Thomas concluded that it was no historical accident that the Logos of God became incarnate in a male, since only males can represent human nature in its integrity.

Thomas insisted no woman could assume leadership in society or the church, and her particular inability to be ordained stemmed logically from this, her defective nature. In both creation and redemption, her position remained secondary and inferior to that of man. Unfortunately, the Protestant Reformation did little to improve the position of women in church and society, and although they expressed it differently, Luther and Calvin shared a similar view of the inferiority of women.[53]

## Alternative Christologies

Androcentric christology, which has obviously dominated the Christian tradition, has been shaped and formulated on the basis of two presuppositions: the male is normative humanity and God is male. In an effort to reassess the relationship of christology to gender and to locate resistance to male hegemony in christological doctrine, Ruether has identified three alternative christological perspectives in the Christian tradition.

1) The Wisdom Tradition    In keeping with her understanding of Christianity as deeply influenced by the Jewish tradition, Ruether identifies an alternative perspective that has non-androcentric possibilities. This perspective is the Wisdom tradition of the Hebrew Scriptures. Although God transcends gender in the Jewish tradition, Ruether points out that God is thought of in terms of sovereignty and power. Such power is expressed through wrath and judgment as well as through compassion and long-suffering. In the Hebrew Scriptures male social roles are predominantly used to image God, but when referring to God's compassion and long-suffering, female images, especially that of a mother, are sometimes used. What is undisputed, however, is that no images of God are to be taken literally. Thus Ruether concludes, "From this tradition it should be clear that the female can be taken as imaging God, while no gender images for God can be taken as literal or exclusive."[54]

Further, in the Wisdom tradition of Hebrew Scripture the presence of God in creation, revelation, and redemption is imaged in the female personification of God's wisdom. According to Ruether, this notion of divine wisdom is the same theological concept expressed in the Christian traditions by the Logos. As a result, she argues, the idea that God's presence among us is restricted to the likeness of a male god, either as parent or "son," cannot be taken literally. According to her, "the Logos-Sophia of God is neither male or female, and was imaged in the major Jewish tradition that lies behind Christian trinitarian thought in female personification."[55] Likewise, in the New Testament the Wisdom tradition offers an alternative possibility for understanding Jesus as God's Sophia or Holy Wisdom. Elizabeth A. Johnson has further developed this:

> Contemporary biblical exegesis has lifted the tradition of personified Wisdom from oblivion and demonstrated convincingly that it played a vital role in early Christian reflection on the creative revelatory and saving signifi-

cance of Jesus of Nazareth. In Paul, Matthew, John and Christian hymns, the characteristics and roles of divine Sophia were applied to Jesus so that he came to be seen and confessed as the embodiment of Sophia herself, the focus of God's gracious presence in the world.[56]

Thus, the Wisdom tradition holds much promise as an alternative resource for a reinterpretation of patriarchal christology.

2) Androgynous Christologies    A second alternative perspective within the Christian tradition Ruether calls "androgynous christologies." Based on the pre-Pauline baptismal formula that in Christ there is neither male nor female because we are all one in Christ (Galatians 3:28), such christologies emphasize the fundamental Christian belief that the whole of human nature, both male and female, is redeemed by Christ. These androgynous christologies see Christ as the symbol and representative of a new humanity in which both male and female are one. The mystical tradition, in particular, has proposed androgynous christologies and sees the dichotomy between maleness and femaleness extinguished on a spiritual level in the community of redeemed humanity. Examples of such androgynous christologies can be found in several Gnostic gospels, medieval mystics such as Julian of Norwich, modern mystics such as Jacob Boehme and Emanuel Swedenborg, and in the efforts of nineteenth century romanticism to feminize Christ and thereby to elevate women to a superior spiritual plane.[57]

Having identified the existence of these androgynous christologies within the tradition, Ruether also evaluates them:

> The very concept of androgynous presupposes a psychic dualism that identifies maleness with one-half of human capacities and femaleness with the other. As long as Christ is still presumed to be, normatively, a male person, androgynous Christologies will carry an androcentric bias. Men gain their "feminine" side, but women contribute to the whole by specializing in the representation of the "feminine" which means exclusion from the exercise of the roles of power and leadership associated with masculinity.[58]

The inherent weakness, then, of these androgynous christologies is that they never succeed in making women as normatively human as men.

3) Spirit Christologies   A third perspective Ruether identifies is that of the "spirit christologies," which took their impetus from Acts 2:18: "Yes, even on my servants and handmaids I will put our a portion of my spirit in those days, and they shall prophesy." In this christological perspective, women as well as men can be instruments, spokespersons and exemplars of Christ. Historically, the earliest expression of this perspective was found in Montanism and in the literature of the martyrs.[59] These positions presupposed that the reality of Christ is ongoing and is revealed in women as well as man, and did not understand Christ as a "past perfect" historical revelation or as a revelation to be embodied in males alone. Such movements led by Joachim of Fiore, Prous Boneta, and Gugliema represented a critique of the clerical church and its closed understanding of Christ and redemption. Movements led by Boneta and Gugliema expected a new age of the Spirit that would include women as spiritual leaders.[60]

The post-Reformation era witnessed th fruit of the earlier Joachite movement in the growth of the Shakers. This group believed in an androgynous God whose feminine side would be liberated and appear at the final coming in the form of a female savior. This savior was expected to usher in the ultimate stage of redemption. A similar idea also was held by other nineteenth century groups such as French utopian socialists and New England Transcendentalists. Mary Baker Eddy's Church of Christ, Scientist also belongs to this genre of religious visionaries. A secular version of this belief in the Joachite prophecy of a new age of the Spirit can be seen in the Enlightenment and in post-Enlightenment radicalism. Although marred by a secular-religious dualism, their efforts to create a new Age of Reason, Ruether claims, was an attempt, among other things, to free people from the superstitious stranglehold of the Christian church. In modern and contemporary times, liberalism, socialism, fascism, and radical feminism are all recent versions of this basically messianic hope for a new age to come, one that would bring liberation, wholeness, and unlimited possibility to both men and women.[61]

## A Feminist Proposal

Ruether maintains that any christology that identifies the maleness of the historical Jesus with normative humanity and with the maleness of God perpetuates misogyny. It also reinforces the second-class status of women in creation, redemption, and the official ministry of the church. Although she gives credit to the creative alternative visions of Wisdom, androgynous, and spirit christologies, she recognizes that they do not solve the problem of formulating a christology that expresses the full personhood of women.[62]

Instead of following one of the alternative christologies, Ruether proposes that the Jesus of the synoptic gospels—rather than the church doctrine that has accumulated around him—be the foundation for a feminist christology. In order to recover the message and praxis of the historical Jesus, we must reject the mythology that portrays him as Messiah or divine Logos, along with the masculine imagery that accompanies these terms. If this is done, we are led to a recognition of Jesus as the iconoclastic prophet who chastised the existing social and religious hierarchies for lording their power over those subject to them. In doing this, Ruether believes, Jesus sought to reverse the social order, making empowerment and the liberation of the oppressed the meaning of servanthood. As a result, Jesus demystified the powerbrokers' use of their leadership and service roles to justify religious and social domination. Using Matthew 23:1-12, Ruether insists that Jesus tried to teach that right relationship with God rejects a dominant-subordinate model in which the relationship between God and human beings is used to justify any type of oppression.[63]

In Jesus' message, his praxis and vision of the Kingdom, women played a particularly important role. Ruether cites his way of dealing with the Samaritan woman, the Syrophoenician women, widows, ritually unclean women, and prostitutes, as examples of the concern Jesus had for the just treatment of women. Ruether argues:

> The role played by women of marginalized groups is an intrinsic part of the iconoclastic, messianic vision. It means that the women are the oppressed of the oppressed. They are the bottom of the present social hierarchy and hence are seen, in a special way, as the last who will be first in the Kingdom of God.[64]

Because Ruether believes Jesus fought against the oppressive "web of status relationships" that characterized the social and religious hierarchies of his day, she insists Jesus is a liberator of all the oppressed, but most especially of poor and lower-class women. She claims that Jesus sought to model a new meaning of right relationship between persons and God and among persons themselves. Such a model was one of mutual empowerment that discouraged any form of service that was dehumanizing.

As "the Christ, the messianic person,"[65] Jesus represented a new humanity in which his maleness "has no ultimate significance."[66] The significance it does have for patriarchal societies is socially symbolic in that

> ...Jesus as the Christ, the representative of liberated humanity and the liberating Word of God, manifests the *kenosis of patriarchy*, the announcement of the new humanity through a lifestyle that discards hierarchical caste privilege and speaks on behalf of the lowly.[67]

Thus, Ruether reasons, that instead of Jesus' biological particularities, we should emphasize his message as expressed in his ministry:

> This message was the revolutionary word of good news to the poor. Good news to the poor means that favor with God and hope of redemption is not based on social status in the hierarchies of unjust society, but is a free grace available to all who respond to it by repenting of their hardness of heart and being open to each other as brothers and sisters. In this perspective we see that the emphasis on Jesus' maleness as essential to his ongoing representation not only is not compatible but is contradictory to the essence of his message as good news to the marginated *qua* women.[68]

Ruether's point, then, is to deemphasize the maleness of Christ and to proclaim instead that "in Christ" a new humanity for both females and males can exist. She suggests that we think of the relationship between redeemer and redeemed in dynamic rather than static terms, and realize that those who have been redeemed are liberated and can, in turn, become vehicles of liberation for others.[69] She concludes:

> Christ, as redemptive person and Word of God, is not to be encapsulated "once-for-all" in the historical Jesus. The Christian community continues Christ's identity. As vine and branches Christic personhood continues in our sisters

and brothers. In the language of early Christian prophe-
tism, we can encounter Christ *in the form of our sister*.
Christ, the liberated humanity, is not confined to a static
perfection of one person two thousand years ago. Rather,
redemptive humanity goes ahead of us, calling us to yet
incomplete dimensions of human liberation.[70]

Here, Ruether's vision of Jesus and the new Christic humanity he
represents challenges contemporary believers. In its most concrete
form this challenge means resisting whatever causes diminishment
to our humanity or anyone else's—especially through patterns of
christology that repudiate persons because of their gender, race, or
religion. It means struggling so that all people are able to receive
their daily bread. It means removing the conditions of indebtedness
we have created for one another. It includes working to deliver the
world from the unjust social structures that are the cause of suffering and death for untold numbers of innocent people. Finally, it
means being open to the divine where the divine has been disal-
lowed, namely, in the experience and imagination of women.[71]

## Conclusions

In a review essay, feminist theologian Carter Heyward states:

...among the most compelling insights emerging currently
among feminist theologians of all colors and different religions is that our theological creativity is enhanced, not
diminished, by understanding the particularities, thus
limits, of our own lives and lived in relation to—not as
identical with—others. Not only our creativity, but also
our moral agency, is strengthened as we struggle to know
and name the relativities and contingencies of our actions
and credos.[72]

Rosemary Radford Ruether is an example of Heyward's statement
and her christological perspective eloquently testifies to this.
Conscious of herself as a women, but also as a member of the dominant race, nation, and religion in today's world, Ruether has been
careful to articulate her theological questions and concerns from
within that awareness. She is keenly sensitive to the "particularities" and "limits" of her life experiences and intellectual journey.
In addition, as a Christian she believes "...God demands a just

world of us...."[73] She has been outstanding in her efforts to respond substantively over the years to two of the most pressing issues facing contemporary christology today: the problem of massive global suffering (particularly that of women) and the legitimacy of extra-Christian religious traditions. The development of her response to these issues is a clear indication of the integrity that underlies her christological perspective.

As noted above, Ruether's christological concerns began as a result of her research around Jewish-Christian relations.[74] Years of study and well-developed personal sensibilities to the plight of the Jewish people have coalesced in her theological agenda. The result is a courageous critique of classical christology, which has raised serious questions about its "saving content." These questions have been raised precisely because, in examining the biblical and philosophical foundations of classical christology, Ruether has laid bare the anti-Judaism inherent in its structure and content. She has also carefully pointed out that by the time of Chalcedon, the influence of Near Eastern, Jewish, and Hellenistic cultures and philosophies combined to shape a brilliant christological synthesis out of the cosmological mythology of the divine Logos. She has concluded that classical christology at its zenith replaced the historical person of Jesus with a cosmological doctrine that issued from contemporary religious philosophy. Ruether is willing to admit that this was both a creative and ingenious effort on the part of "the Fathers" to make sense of Jesus from within the historical and cultural circumstances that conditioned them. Nonetheless, she insists that christology must be situated in the total context of its historical development so that today we can better perceive what it originally meant. Only then will we be able to ask what it might mean in our contemporary world, in relation not only to Jews, but to other religions and groups of people heretofore victimized by oppressive christological formulations and their effects.[75]

Because Ruether's theology is characterized by a concern for those suffering under traditional christologies, her critique includes not only a denunciation of the suffering inflicted upon Jewish people by traditional doctrine, but also how doctrine has simultaneously promoted sexism, racism, and imperialism. At the same time, her critique is an affirmation of those "others," those people whose gender, history, culture, and religious sensibilities profoundly challenge the dominant christological formulations.

Her critique stems from her keen awareness that all these "others," along with nature itself, are victims of the same white, Western, male, Christian god.

I propose that it is Ruether's most recent articulation of a feminist christology that most inclusively addresses the issues of global suffering and the validity of extra-Christian religious experience.[76] Her christology demands that the experience of both men *and* women, members of various religious traditions, people of color and those in the less dominant nations of the world be acknowledged and respected in any credible contemporary christological formulation. Therefore, Ruether's feminist christology proposes that Christ be understood as a paradigm of liberated humanity. This results, on a practical level, in recognizing the incarnation as inclusive of both genders, as well as of all races and historical conditions. Such recognition makes it impossible for males to continue to claim that they more truly represent Christ than females do. It also more readily embraces the validity of non-white and non-Western religious perceptions of Christ and asserts that christology must be divorced from a hierarchical, philosophical, cosmological perspective that sanctions the status quo. Instead, any credible christology must be revelatory of Jesus, who, in God's name, denounced religious ideologies that—under the guise of being the will of God—justify oppressive structures. The result of this for women is an end to male hegemony in the church and an elimination of the male-designated roles that have marked women as subordinate and inferior. A further result and goal for members of extra-Christian religious traditions, people of color, and Third World peoples is the dethronement of the racist, classist, and imperialist assumption that the god who sits at the top of this inviolable chain of being is also, unquestionably, white, Western, middle-class, and Christian.

Ruether's christology also demands that a past historical Jesus no longer be understood as the only model of Christ. As the paradigm of liberated and redeemed humanity, Jesus preached the Kingdom on behalf of the poor and oppressed. He embodied a new vision of human existence, one marked by mutuality and reciprocity. We are therefore called to model him in our relationships with one another. "That means that, here and now, we encounter Christ not only in the past Jesus, but in our sisters (and brothers) today as well."[77] Such a vision expands our imaginations and frees us to be open particularly to "...a primal re-encounter with divine reality...that gives birth to new stories and therefore new foundations for women's identity and understanding of God."[78] Although Ruether's feminist christology is directed against christological formulations that denigrate and oppress women, it is also a fundamental affirmation of women's experience of Christ.

It is my contention that, deeply motivated as she is by an "ethic of solidarity,"[79] Ruether's feminist christology can be liberating not only for women, but also for members of other faith traditions, people of color, and those beyond the Western hemisphere. It is also my belief that, given her identification with those most victimized in our world today, Ruether's feminist christology will continue to manifest further development and integration as her own life experiences, choices, and intellectual journey unfold.

Ruether's christology is a courageous attempt to respond, in both theory and praxis, to the suffering and pluralism that characterize our world today. On the one hand, her proposal clearly denounces the evil distortions of orthodox christology; on the other hand, it affirms the religious integrity of all people (particularly Jews), and demands that the full personhood of women be recognized. It seeks to affirm and sustain the ecological harmony of the universe, and in solidarity with Latin and Central America liberation theologies, it also testifies to an understanding of the historical Jesus whose actions revealed a preferential option for the poor and oppressed. In the final analysis, her christological proposal challenges us to address the most critical question facing every contemporary christological formulation: What does it *do* and *for whom*?

# Questions for Reflection and Discussion

1. Consonant with Third World liberation theologians, Ruether argues that christology must be rooted in the historical person Jesus. What have you been taught about Jesus as a historical person?

2. Does your knowledge of the historical Jesus support or contradict

what Ruether and Third World liberation theologians are calling for with respect to the starting point for christology?

3. What was Jesus' vision fo the kingdom of God, according to Ruether? Where do you see that vision being taken seriously today?

4. What is the relationship between the theological and sociopolitical implications of Ruether's christology and conversion?

5. Discuss Ruether's proposal for a renewed ecological perspective within Christianity.

6. According to Ruether, what is the authentic interpretation of Logos christology? How did this interpretation become distorted?

7. Explain Ruether's proposal for a feminist christology.

8. Share your vision of "church" in light of Ruether's feminist christology.

# ♉ CHAPTER 4

## Christological Issues: Raised and Debated

The purpose of this chapter is to situate Rosemary Radford Ruether among other North American Roman Catholic theologians who are raising some of the same christological issues she is. Some of these issues are: christology, Judaism and Interreligious Dialogue, christology and Third World liberation theology, christology and the uniqueness of Christ, christology and women, christology and ecology, and christology and the tradition. The theologians I have chosen for comparison are Monika Hellwig, Paul Knitter, and William M. Thompson.[1] All have evidenced a pastoral concern for the many who are suffering in our world today as well as a concern for the issue of interreligious dialogue from a christological perspective. Unlike Ruether, Hellwig has raised the issue of christology and fidelity to the tradition in a comprehensive way. Knitter has emphasized the issue of christology and the uniqueness of Jesus, and Thompson has provided a creative proposal regarding christology and ecology. Whereas all four do not treat each one of these issues explicitly, each issue is directly or indirectly at the center of their christological concerns and the contemporary christological debate.

## Christology, Judaism, and Interreligious Dialogue: Rosemary Radford Ruether and Monika K. Hellwig

I have demonstrated the extent to which Jewish-Christian relations are formative in the development of Ruether's christology. Another North American theologian who has been involved in the Jewish-Christian dialogue is Monika Hellwig. Both women acknowledge that traditional christological formulations have fostered Christian anti-Judaism, but they disagree about the extent of it and about how the situation may be remedied.

Ruether has argued that "theologically, anti-Judaism developed as the lefthand of christology," that Christian understandings of the Christ are rooted in religious bigotry toward the Jews.[2] In an attempt to address this issue, Hellwig has criticized Ruether's book, *Faith and Fratricide: The Theological Roots of Anti-Semitism*.[3] From the very beginning of her review it is clear that Hellwig considers Ruether's critique of christology vis a vis Judaism to be strident, unorthodox, and iconoclastic.[4] Nonetheless, Hellwig agrees that some christological reformulation is necessary. Initially, in response to Ruether, Hellwig argues that Christian interpretation of the title "Messiah" is radically different from the Hebrew usage of the term and claims all credible theologians admit this. She does not consider this to be an issue between Christians and Jews. Nor does she focus on other issues that Ruether raises: realized eschatology, anti-Judaic dualisms, Christian interpretation of the Hebrew Scriptures, or religious imperialism. For Hellwig the issue that undergirds the division between Christians and Jews is the understanding of redemption found within the Christian claim.[5]

According to Hellwig, the early followers of Jesus claimed to have had an already realized experience of salvation that was reflected in the personal and communal dimensions of their lives.

> Jesus is acclaimed as divine saviour, as the self-utterance of God in history, as the Divine Word that is the pattern of creation as well as redemption, because of the utter and self-validating simplicity of the reintegration of broken human persons, broken human history, the broken human world, as experienced by Christians in the following of Jesus of Nazareth.[6]

Further, she denies that this belief led Christianity to spiritualize the notion of salvation, that is, insist it has nothing to do with the concrete historical needs of people as they seek to become fully human. Rather, she claims that Jesus is seen as savior because through him the promises made to Israel have been universalized. "The cumulative effect of this is that the Christian claim of salvation in Jesus as the Christ is linked to a universalized notion of peoplehood."[7] This notion, in Hellwig's estimation, does not deserve charges of supersession [superiority] in terms of Israel's election and peoplehood. Jewish and Christian understandings of election and peoplehood are not antithetical, according to her, because the Jewish understanding is particular and historical, while the Christian understanding is universal and other-worldly.

> Rather the antithesis appears because both are highly particular and this-worldly in the way they are rooted in history and in those historical experiences that have been in some measure self-validating experiences of salvation. The people of Israel is not seen as central to the history of salvation because there is a center elsewhere. That center is not simply Jesus of Nazareth, Jew of his time with universal significance for the gentiles. That center is the enchurched and even domesticated Christ figure that has accumulated a great deal of unacknowledged cultural accretion since Chalcedon. In the light of the whole historical sequence, it becomes much clearer why Jews of our time frequently see an antithesis between the Christ of Christianity and the Jewish commitment to Israel, while maintaining at the same time that they do not see the same conflict between the historical Jesus and the fate of his people in history.[8]

According to Hellwig, if the issue of supersession is to be resolved between Christians and Jews, the contemporary christological task is one of disentanglement and reformulation that is faithful to the tradition. For christological dogmas cannot be understood by examination of the dogmatic definitions alone. A study of the imagery and story that express the experience and devotion of the followers of Jesus must also be included. Therefore, it is both the historical Jesus and the story of the salvation experienced through him by his followers that must constitute the Christ of dogma.[9]

From this perspective Hellwig argues that it has not been shown by Ruether that anti-Semitism is rooted in the essential structures of Christian doctrine: christology. Nor does she feel it can be shown. Secondly, Hellwig is certain that Christian anti-Semitism can be corrected within the tradition. She acknowledges that hostility, apathy and self-interest will certainly block the process. Nevertheless, the history of Christianity also includes the capacity for self-criticism in the development of its doctrine. Such a process Hellwig is convinced, will continue in the future as it has in the past.[10]

It is in this light that Hellwig suggests some new directions for reformulating christological doctrine in a Roman Catholic context. These are three: that christological proposals be inclusive rather than exclusive, ascending rather than descending, and concerned with recovering the socio-political dimensions of Christian hope.[11] Drawing from this, she makes a tentative proposal for the theoretical construction of a Roman Catholic christological perspective that substantially differs from what Ruether has proposed, given Ruether's critique of Jewish-Christian relations.

Hellwig's proposal includes, first of all, continuity with Chalcedon with modifications in its approach and vocabulary. Secondly, this proposal maintains the unique role and place of Jesus in history, while acknowledging Christianity's indebtedness to Judaism which made the Christ-event possible. Lastly, her proposal challenges the "unquestioned ethnocentric assumptions" that have led Christians to claim covenantal superiority over Israel.

She further states that new questions arising out of the ongoing historical experience of Christianity challenge the old unquestioned assumptions and test whether they are, in fact, true reflections of the saving power and mercy of Jesus. Examples of these "new questions" are Auschwitz and the state of Israel. In addition, there are the questions posed by the voices of the poor, oppressed, and marginalized whose suffering impels Christians to clarify what they understand by salvation. According to Hellwig, this is the context for Jewish-Christian dialogue. Here Christian confession of Jesus as divine savior emerges as a "friendly wager," that God is truly and uniquely revealed in Jesus for the salvation of all. Implicit in all of this for Hellwig is that such a wager will someday prove self-evident in the concrete life and praxis of the Christian community.[12]

Ruether has responded briefly to Hellwig's critique of *Faith and Fratricide*. She admits that Hellwig recognizes that there is a connection between traditional christological formulations and Christian anti-Judaism, but faults Hellwig for attempting to reformulate christology in a way that disavows this anti-Judaism. Further, Ruether claims that Hellwig believes in a formula of parallel covenantal communities, each with its own positive salvational principles, and that as far as the church is concerned, its acceptance of Jesus as the Christ is a revelation that both fulfills and completes Judaism. In the final analysis, as far as Ruether is concerned, Hellwig's assessment of what divides Jews from Christians does not probe sufficiently the presence of anti-Judaism in the foundations of Christian faith.[13]

In a more recent christological essay, *Jesus the Compassion of God*, Hellwig addresses the issue of christology not only from the perspective of Judaism, but also with regard to Buddhism, Islam, and the thought of Gandhi. She discusses issues such as the divinity claim, Jesus as the final revelation of God, and the relation between the law and liberation. With regard to Buddhism she explores the salvation claims made for both Christ and the Buddha. In addition, she compares the life of Gandhi with that of Jesus as the Compassion of God in order to challenge Christians to act on behalf of justice (as Gandhi did). Although Hellwig is deeply respectful of each tradition and what it has to offer Christianity, she seems to hold on to the superiority of Jesus in relation to other savior figures. For example, in the context of the Buddha and Jesus she states, "Yet to claim only that Jesus offers a way of salvation to us, which is one among many, is to fall short of fidelity to the classic statements about Jesus in the Bible and the tradition."[14] At the same time, however, she also suggests, with regard to Christianity, Judaism, and Islam, that all three traditions, "...in principle...might be right and that this would be eschatologically evident in a retrospective observation of the convergence of the substance, if not the religious language and observances, of the traditions."[15]

Hellwig formulates her christological proposal *prior* to any serious discussion of christology vis-a-vis other religions. Thus, Hellwig's christological proposal is not substantially affected by the objections extra-Christian religious traditions make concerning Christian claims for Jesus as the unique, divine, and final mediator of universal salvation.[16] Ruether's main focus is on christology with regard to Judaism, but her proposal offers more possibility for further dialogue with members of other faith traditions than does Hellwig's.[17]

The key aspects in this issue for Ruether are, initially, to develop a christological formulation that is nonnormative or, in her own terms, paradigmatic and proleptic—one not based solely on a past historical Jesus. This is to avoid attributing an exclusivist finality to Christ and the church that, among other things, inhibits interreligious dialogue. Although Hellwig supports an inclusive christological proposal, she is not willing to concede that traditional christological formulations have damaged Jewish-Christian relations to the extent that Ruether claims.

Second, Ruether supports removing Jesus Christ from the center of history, and argues that an understanding of Jesus as the center of history has led to attitudes of superiority and intolerance among Christians. Under this arrogance anti-Judaism has flourished. Such a "paradigm shift," Ruether argues, can keep Christians more active on behalf of the kingdom which has not yet arrived. It would also allow for new understandings of the Christ to develop as religious peoples share the common commitment to fostering a more human world order.

Hellwig would not support such a paradigm shift. She suggests that understanding Jesus as the Compassion of God can alleviate tensions between Christians and members of other faith traditions, for it implies movement into the experience of "the other" and action on their behalf against injustice. It seems to me that Ruether would support her proposal in this regard, however, she would also argue that Hellwig's very insistence on fidelity to the classical tradition prevents her proposal of Jesus as the Compassion of God from becoming the vehicle of solidarity she anticipates it might be.

Both women, however, would agree that orthopraxis is essential to any credible contemporary christological proposal.

> The "truth" of dogma and tradition must constantly be exposed to the "ultimate arbiter" of truth—that is, "the transformative response of Christian praxis." "Right knowing" (orthodoxy) without "right doing" (orthopraxis) does not exist.[18]

In the area of interreligious dialogue this position rejects any christological perspective that fosters a supersessionist or imperialistic approach to extra-Christian religious traditions. Ultimately, much more dialogue on this issue of christology and religious intolerance is required, for at stake in the dialogue is unity among humankind in the face of massive global suffering and the destruction of the earth.

## Christology and Third World Liberation Theology: Rosemary Radford Ruether and Paul F. Knitter

As stated earlier, Ruether is a staunch supporter of liberation theology.[19] Specifically, she has supported liberation theologians in their claim that the most basic characteristic of Jesus' message and praxis is that it reveals a preferential option for the poor and oppressed: "...following Christ's identification with the poor by seeking to transform the social structures that generate deprivation and dehumanization."[20] Likewise with liberation theologians, she claims that Jesus' vision of the Kingdom was historical and material, beginning in this world with every effort to overcome poverty, injustice, and oppression. Such an understanding of Jesus and his vision of the Kingdom requires Christians to be in active solidarity with the most vulnerable and marginalized in our world today.

Like Ruether, Paul Knitter is also a strong supporter of liberation theology. In tandem with the "ethical hermeneutics" of First World theologians such as Ruether, Knitter has analyzed the methodological contribution of Latin American liberation theologians in terms of his initial proposal for a theocentric model of christology.[21] Knitter, however, has expanded his understanding of the contribution liberation theology can play within the context of interreligious dialogue. This is evidenced by his shift from a "theocentric" model of religions to a "soteriocentric" liberative model.

> Theologians of religions must begin to listen to theologians of liberation. It is, I suggest the preferential option for the poor and non-person—i.e., the praxis of human, socio-economic liberation—that today can best provide a common ground and goal for dialogue, a new hermeneutical situation and possibility of mutual understanding. If, as I argue in the book, there has been in Christian approaches to other faiths an evolution from ecclesiocentrism to chris-

tocentrism to theocentrism, it is now time to move to sote-riocentrism.[22]

Knitter further explains what this shift means:

> This understanding of the central role of the preferential option for the poor and nonpersons within interreligious dialogue means that the evolution within Christian atti-tudes toward other faiths that I described in my book *No Other Name?* is incomplete. The evolution, I suggest, is being called to a further stage. If Christian attitudes have evolved from ecclesiocentrism to christocentrism to theocentrism, they must now move on to what in Christian symbols might be called "kingdom-centrism," or more uni-versally, "soteriocentrism." For Christians, that which constitutes the basis and the goal for interreligious dia-logue, that which makes mutual understanding and coop-eration between the religions possible...that which unites the religions in common discourse and praxis is *not* how they are related to the church...or how they are related to Christ..., nor even how they respond to and conceive of God, but rather, to what extent they are promoting *soteria* (in Christian images, the basileia)—to what extent they are engaged in promoting human welfare and bringing about liberation with and for the poor and nonpersons.[23]

This shift to "soteriocentrism" is grounded in Knitter's urgent belief that the "signs of the times" i.e., "the experience of the many poor and the experience of the many religions," require it.[24] According to him, the theology of liberation and the theology of religions need each other to effectively transform our suffering world.

Knitter proposes three ways in which a liberation theology of religions can illuminate theologians engaged in interreligious dia-logue:

1) By incorporating a "hermeneutics of suspicion" into their methodologies, theologians of religion can more honestly examine their traditions and doctrines for any evidence of a desire to domi-nate, control, or devalue other religious traditions.[25]

2) By making the preferential option for the poor and oppressed the "common context and starting point" for interreligious dialogue, theologians of religion can more easily avoid ideological God-talk

and simultaneously uphold a shared soteriological thrust among the religions for global liberation of the suffering poor.

3) By adopting praxis, the concrete efforts to transform a suffering world, as a constitutive methodological requirement, theologians of religions can utilize it as the norm for judging or grading the authenticity of any doctrine of practice among the world religions.

These three contributions from the theology of liberation that Knitter has cited, namely, a "hermeneutics of suspicion," the preferential option for the poor and oppressed, and the primacy of praxis, have been key methodological concerns of Ruether's with regard to christological doctrine, particularly as they call attention to the global suffering of women. In light of this she would agree with Knitter that Third World liberation theology has much to offer a theology of religions. However, she would insist such dialogue must include "... women's experiences of agony and victimization, survival, empowerment, and new life, as place of divine presence...."[26] No longer can interreligious dialogue fail to make women's experience, specifically their experience of suffering and victimization, central to its conversations.

> Feminists must create a new midrash on scripture or a "Third Testament" that can tell stories of God's presence in experiences where God's presence was never allowed or imagined before in a religous culture controlled by men and defined by male experience. This Third Testament is not simply a religion for women. Just as women have been able to experience themselves in the crucified rabbi from Nazareth, men must be able to experience Christ in the raped woman and thereby come to experience the question mark this directs at a male culture in which the tortured female body is regarded as pornographic, rather than the expression of the sufferings of God.[27]

Further, Ruether's feminist perspective on this issue expands the traditional boundaries of interreligious dialogue:

> This new feminist midrash on patriarchal texts and traditions will not only enter into dialogue and controversy with patriarchal religion. It must also open itself to dialogue with feminist exploration of religion in other traditions. There must certainly be a dialogue between Chris-

tian and Jewish feminists, and also with Muslim feminists as well. There must also be a dialogue between feminists engaged in the transformation of historical religions and feminists who break with these historical religions and seek to revive, from repressed memories of ancient goddesses and burned witches, visions of new possibilities for women's spirituality today.[28]

Thus, Ruether would urge that the three methodological contributions of liberation theology must include women's experiences of victimization and empowerment as loci of divine revelation. Simultaneously, she would add that a liberation theology of religion must also include the perspectives of feminists within both historical and pagan religious traditions.

There is no doubt that Third World liberation theology has had a significant impact on the development of the christological perspectives of Rosemary Radford Ruether and Paul Knitter, concerned as each is about the status of interreligious dialogue and those who are suffering most in our world. Conversations about these issues must be ongoing. As Knitter himself has stated, "...the task of christology, of interpreting the Christ event is never finished."[29] Certainly Ruether would agree.

## Christology and the Uniqueness of Jesus: Rosemary Radford Ruether and Paul F. Knitter

Only twice does Ruether specifically use the word "unique" in relation to Jesus. In both cases she argues against making a claim of uniqueness for him. According to her, the statement, "Jesus is the Christ" makes sense only insofar as it is an affirmation that is "...paradigmatic for the structure of human existence and not something unique about Jesus."[30] In light of this I would argue that Ruether does not support traditional claims for the uniqueness of Jesus, either an exclusive or inclusive uniqueness.[31]

To begin with, Ruether claims that Jesus did not think of himself as "the last Word" or the "once-for-all" disclosure of God. Rather, she insists that he pointed beyond himself to One still to come. She also argues that Christians must refuse any closed model of christology that makes the past historical Jesus the only and exclusive model of Christ. Instead, she maintains that Jesus must be seen as a paradigm of redeemed humanity, who, by announcing the Kingdom, announced not himself, but a liberated humanity yet to come. This redemptive paradigm, which Jesus' life and praxis embodied, continues in the collective life of the Christian community. To live out of this paradigm, then, is what it means to live "in Christ," in the new humanity which Jesus neither completed nor exhausted but yet pointed to as a coming reality beyond himself.[32]

Ruether raises several provocative questions in light of the issue of Jesus' uniqueness, one of which is the following:

> As our perception of our incompleteness changes with new sensitivities to racism, sexism, and European chauvinism, must not the image of Christ take ever new forms: as woman, as Black and Brown woman, as impoverished and despised woman of those peoples who are the underside of Christian imperialism?[33]

Such a question makes it clear that Ruether upholds neither a *constitutive* nor a *normative* understanding of the uniqueness of Jesus. Rather, she is more closely aligned with the concept of the "complementary uniqueness" of Jesus that Paul Knitter proposes.

Through his shift from a theocentric model for a Christian theology of the religions to a soteriocentric model, Paul Knitter has readdressed the issue of christology and the uniqueness of Jesus. Utilizing the three methodological contributions of liberation theology mentioned above, he makes several suggestions for dealing with this issue.

First, he argues for the centrality of praxis in confirming, clarifying and correcting christological doctrine.

> In other words, the Christian conviction and proclamation that Jesus is God's final and normative word for all religions cannot rest only on traditional doctrine *or* on personal, individual experience. We cannot know that Jesus is God's last or normative statement only on the basis of being told so or on the basis of having experienced him to be such in our own lives. Rather, the uniqueness of Jesus can be know and then affirmed only "in its concrete embodiment," only in the praxis of historical, social involvement. This means, concretely, that unless we are engaged in the *praxis of Christian dialogue* with other religions—within the dialogue

with other believers—we cannot experience and confirm what the uniqueness and normativity of Christ mean.[34]

From Knitter's point of view the perspective that Jesus is the unique and definitive revelation of God for all religions precludes the possibility of engaging in interreligious dialogue.

Second, Knitter suggests that the preferential option for the poor and oppressed is a critical tool which can be used to evaluate and revise, if necessary, traditional understandings of the uniqueness of Christ, as well as to "grade" other salvific figures in the world's religions. In this approach all religious paths and their saviors are judged on the basis of how much or how little they contribute to promoting global justice. Thus, "Jesus would then be unique—together with other unique liberators. He would be universal savior—with other universal saviors. His universality and uniqueness would be not exclusive nor inclusive, but complimentary."[35]

Third, in his soteriocentric approach to the uniqueness of Christ, Knitter upholds the primacy of orthopraxis over orthodoxy. He maintains "right practice" in furthering the salvific message and deeds of Jesus takes precedence over "right belief" in light of the urgent needs of the world's poor and oppressed. To effect the reception of a nondefinitive, nonabsolutist understanding of the uniqueness of Christ with the faithful in the Christian churches, Knitter reiterates the basic liberationist tenet that orthopraxis must hold primacy over orthodoxy. He insists that by challenging the faithful to affirm the primacy of orthopraxis, these new views of Jesus' "complementary uniqueness" can enable them to deepen their Christian commitment. This is possible, he argues, because most Christians recognize that the essence of being a Christian is doing God's will rather than simply believing in Jesus as the definitive revelation of God.[36]

According to Knitter, recognizing the primacy of orthopraxis over orthodoxy will also enable Christians to better comprehend New Testament language as "action language" calling Christians to embrace Jesus' message and vision of the kingdom rather than merely to adhere to a set of doctrinal beliefs about him. Thus, Knitter proposes that "if recognizing the possibility of other saviors or mediators does not impede this praxis, then it is compatible with Christian identity and tradition."[37]

Ruether, who like Knitter does not support traditional claims for the uniqueness of Jesus, would also agree with him that praxis must be the starting point in formulating christological doctrine, that "right practice" must indeed take precedence over "right belief."

Further, she would argue, Jesus' uniqueness lies *not* in his onto-logical structure, but in his role as liberator which he expressed in his message and praxis, that is, his ministry. As liberator, Jesus modeled a new kind of humanity wherein he called for a renuncia-tion and termination of the "web of status relationships" by which societies defined those who would have power and privi-lege and those who would not. In doing this, he rejected a system of domination and sought to embody a new humanity character-ized by service, mutuality, and empowerment. So too, the unique-ness of his ministry became a "revolutionary word of good news to the poor."[38]

> Good news to the poor means that favor with God and hope of redemption is not based on social status in the hierar-chies of unjust society, but is a free grace available to all who respond to it by repenting of their hardness of heart and being open to each other as brothers and sisters.[39]

It is this "ethical hermeneutic" that Knitter acknowledges from Ruether and other First World theologians as a methodological contribution to reinterpreting the uniqueness of Jesus. In other words, the truth of any christological statement must be judged by its ethical fruits. If a particular belief in Christ either causes or condones a practice that is considered unethical from Christian moral standards, then something is wrong with that belief. Thus, for Ruether and Knitter, in his role as liberator, expressed in his message and ministry of good news to the poor and oppressed, Jesus is a unique and paradigmatic expression of God's Logos-Sophia for the Christian community.[40] When christological formulations fail to include or contradict this in any way, they must be rejected.

Ruether is in agreement with Knitter on several other points with regard to this issue. They have similar perspectives regard-ing the tension between universality and particularity. Both sup-port a historically conscious worldview rather than a classicist mentality that views truth as a matter of either-or. Finally, both have adopted what H. Richard Niebuhr refers to as a "confes-sional" stance toward christology.[41] Such a stance affirms: "In boldly proclaiming that God has indeed been defined in Jesus,

Christians will also humbly admit that God has not been confined to Jesus."[42] Further dialogue in the Christian community is undoubtedly needed to test the perspectives on the uniqueness of Jesus, offered by both Ruether and Knitter.

## Christology and Women:
## Rosemary Radford Ruether and Monika K. Hellwig

With regard to the issue of women and christology, Rosemary Radford Ruether has denounced the misogyny and androcentrism embedded in the christological tradition; a closed model of christology based on a "past perfect" understanding of Jesus that presupposes God is most fully revealed in a white, middle-class male; and a philosophical, cosmological, and hierarchical christological perspective that sanctifies the status quo. In turn, she has affirmed that the message and praxis of Jesus should be the basis for a liberating christological perspective (with regard to women in particular) rather than any emphasis on his biological particularities. Such a praxis-based christology is significant methodologically insofar as it supports only those formulations inclusive of the full personhood of women. Ruether has also affirmed a perspective that is open to new understandings of Christ, especially those revealed in women's experience and has insisted Christians be open to encountering Christ "in the form of our sister."

In her christological proposal of Jesus as the Compassion of God, Monika Hellwig does not include a discussion of women and christology. Although it is evident that she is deeply concerned about those who suffer most in this world, she does not employ any explicit feminist critique. Nevertheless, I offer two points for reflection in light of this. Initially, I would argue, Hellwig is in methodological agreement with Ruether. Both maintain that orthopraxis is key in determining the integrity of any contemporary christological statement, i.e., any belief in Christ that proves oppressive or denigrating to any segment of humanity must be rejected. Unlike Ruether though, Hellwig does not apply this methodological presupposition specifically to the plight of women.

Secondly, by naming Jesus as the compassion of God, Hellwig, like Ruether, does emphasize his ministry rather than his biological particularities. Certainly Hellwig's understanding of compassion as participation in the experience of the other and action on behalf of the other against suffering and oppression includes women. The failure to explicitly name women as victims of past christological formulations is less a christological issue for Hellwig than it is an ecclesial one. She seeks to serve the ecclesial community which she distinguishes from the ecclesiastical hierarchy. In this community her concern is poor women. In my opinion, Hellwig believes that U.S. feminism and feminist theology do not seriously address the needs of these women, nor their relationship to the church. Therefore she distances herself from the feminist critique in order "to be of service to the little people."[43] Thus, it seems to be a question of strategy for Hellwig in light of her self-understanding as an ecclesial woman.

Further dialogue would be useful between these two scholars given the import of this issue and the respective impact each wields in fostering justice-making for women in the Roman Catholic church.

## Christology and Ecology: Rosemary Radford Ruether and William M. Thompson

In agreement with the respected North American theologian, William Thompson, Rosemary Ruether affirms that, while it would be invalid to claim that Jesus possessed an ecological consciousness such as we have today, it is not invalid to suggest there is an ecological dimension to his teachings. These can be found both in his high view of nature and in what Thompson calls Jesus' ethics of self-limiting love and respect for creation.[44] For Thompson, Jesus' ethics of self-limitation is seen as "...his refusal to exploit and harm anyone or anything."[45]

Thompson suggests that "the real ecological originality of the Jesus event resides in the vision and praxis of the new community (or Kingdom) as the end of exploitation, the overcoming of the oppressor-oppressed dialectic...."[46] Further, he claims that the divine love, justice, and peace that Jesus revealed, if carried in "sympathetic followers," promotes a "covenantal harmony" among people and with respect to the environment. Similarly, Ruether has shown that Jesus' vision of redemption flows from the Hebrew prophetic sense that there is one covenant of creation which includes a harmonious relationship between nature and society.

In addition, although each theologian develops the notion of dualistic thinking somewhat differently, both Thompson and Ruether have identified dualism as one important factor in the Christian tradition that accounts for attitudes of distrust and denigration toward the material world. This dualism, which opposes the transcendent-spiritual dimensions of life to the natural-material, is especially noted in negative attitudes toward the body and sexuality, and in an attitude that abuses nature for materialistic and technological ends.[47]

Ruether's understanding of the lordship of Christ as servanthood incorporates the way Christians relate to nature.[48] The lordship of Christ (understood as servanthood) means an end to domination of any kind. This includes the tyranny human beings have exercised over the natural world in the unbridled technological "development" that has laid waste our land and polluted our lakes, rivers, and cities. Thus, Ruether would support Thompson's concept of Jesus' ethics of self-limitation as a way to further develop the connection between christology and ecology. According to Thompson:

> Jesus' ethics of self-limitation calls for a new form of asceticism for the future which must find social and even global embodiment as an asceticism of care for the body and bodily and ecological health. In other words, a Jesus-inspired ethics seeks to build up the true covenant intended for us by God, a covenant of harmony in which exploitation no longer reigns.[49]

Thompson cites the need for ongoing conversion from self-centeredness to the values and praxis of the Kingdom if this "covenantal harmony" is to be established. This is similar to Ruether's emphasis on conversion as the way to develop a just and balanced society characterized by a harmonious relationship between human beings and the natural world. Such conversion of the heart, both would agree, can lead to a proper use of technology and a reverential respect for nature.

In agreement with Ruether's perspective, Thompson recognizes the connection between the exploitation of nature and violence toward women. He argues that this connection must be considered as a necessary step toward authentic conversion. For, "the hidden link between misogynism and ecological imbalance is the heart perverted by exploitation, which then finds embodiment in abusive social and natural interrelations."[50] Consequently, Thompson proposes an ecologically sensitive dimension to christology on two levels, personal and societal. On a personal level he suggests that a conversion to a vision and praxis of ecological harmony involves repentance from a self-gratifying lifestyle that limitlessly exploits both body and environment. Such personal conversion will demand faith in the possibilities that a balanced and harmonious universe offer. On a societal level, he urges conversion as the "key task," taking his cue from the psycho-social critics, among whom he numbers Ruether. These critics caution against viewing an ethics of self-limitation too privatistically. Not only personal, but collective detachment must be embraced in order to terminate the actions and attitudes that promote the rape of nature. There is, after all, a systemic connection between self-exploitation, societal exploitation, the exploitation of nature, and our disoriented relation to the divine.[51]

Both Ruether and Thompson offer an alternative vision for an ecologically healthy relationship between humankind and nature based on their understanding of Jesus as one who sought harmony and justice for all. Such visions offer hope and promise that Christians will choose life instead of destruction for the already ravaged universe where the human is but one of thousands of species that has been entrusted to our keeping.

## Christology and the Tradition: Rosemary Radford Ruether and Monika K. Hellwig

Ruether is faithful to the tradition as long as it does not, in her estimation, contradict Jesus' message and praxis or the interpretation of him made by the early Christian community as presented in the gospels.[52] When she ascertains that any aspect of the tradition is unfaithful to this she does not include it in her christological perspective. Such is the case with regard to Nicaea, Chalcedon and their subsequent interpretations. Ruether has admitted that the classical formulation was a brilliant synthesis, given the pervasive turmoil and complexity that surrounded its development. She also admits, particularly with regard to Chalcedon, that it *could* have been interpreted differently: that the lordship of Christ is a judgment on the oppressive hierarchies of this world rather than the source and confirmation of them. However, she claims this was not Chalcedon's tendency and the result has been a sacralization of established hierarchical systems and the imperialism, sexism, racism, and classism they provoked.

Ruether's critique of classical christology has made it possible for many women to *name* the oppression foisted upon them by such concepts as the maleness of God, the Logos and the *imago dei*. Likewise, she has opened innumerable eyes to the pervasive anti-Judaism present in classical formulations. Significantly, her critique has also called attention to the relationship that should exist between christology and ethics: she has insisted that what we say we believe about Jesus Christ as Savior must bear fruit in the way we relate to one another, especially the vulnerable and marginalized among us.

Simultaneously, her critique of the tradition has led her to insist that women's experience of the divine be recognized as a valid insight into the infinite reality of God. So, too, this same critique has exposed the possibility and promise of encountering Christ "in the form of our sister." She has also challenged us to see Jesus as a paradigm of liberated humanity, inviting us to recognize the incarnation as inclusive of both genders, as well as all races, creeds, and historical conditions.

Finally, her critique of classical christology denounces a hierarchical, cosmological perspective that upholds the status quo and suggests that we no longer understand a past historical Jesus as the only model of Christ. Such a perspective dethrones the white, middle-class male god that has dominated the tradition. Indeed, it opens the door to new models of Christ in a community that understands redemption to be ongoing and incomplete at this point in history.

Monika Hellwig takes quite a different approach to the classical tradition. She sees Chalcedon as a marker along the way, while Ruether sees it as a roadblock. Hellwig is adamant that, in order to be taken seriously by communities of believers, current christological formulations must maintain their congruence with Chalcedon, which, in her view, is a criterion of orthodoxy, an enduring reference point of departure for all christological speculation. Acknowledging that Chalcedon's primary intent was to defend the true humanity of Jesus, Hellwig sees the formulation as a valuable expression of faith, for it represents centuries of doctrinal development and is based on the liturgical and devotional formulae of the time.

Simultaneously, she defends the Chalcedonian authors' use of concepts and categories that reflect a Greek philosophical world-view by claiming that their concern was to instruct adult converts to the Christian faith. Such an intention demanded a reshaping of consciousness, identity, and worldview from pagan to Christian understanding. To accomplish this the authors' utilized language, symbolism, and imagery that would be relevant to the life experience of the people of their era.[53]

As unflinchingly loyal as Hellwig is to Chalcedon, she is not without her criticisms of it from a contemporary christological perspective. She has cited difficulty with the philosophical background of Chalcedon, along with the language, symbolism, and categories that comprise its formulations. The lack of a historical understanding of the development of the doctrinal formulations along with the retention of a vocabulary that conveys static meaning under diverse historical conditions make Chalcedon difficult to use in current christological speculation.[54]

Insightfully, Hellwig has pointed out that there are serious and negative social implications conveyed by the Chalcedonian formulation:

> [Jesus'] character as universal mediator of salvation is already assured by his prior divine identity, yielding a Christology in which the doctrine of the Incarnation renders life, preaching, passion, death and resurrection all rather peripheral to the significance of Jesus, that is, to the difference that he makes in the history of the human community. This is a severe problem to Christian believers because they consider themselves followers or imitators of Jesus. It suggests that the perfect model of what is human before God is that of inactivity. If the redemptive event was that the human nature of Jesus was assumed by the divine prior to any human decision, then it is reasonable to conclude that one becomes party to the realm of the divine Jesus, the realm of grace, prior to any human decision or response. Anything that follows in lifestyle, action, personal commitment and so forth would tend to be peripheral.[55]

Finally, Hellwig has noted that the Chalcedonian formulation arises from an experience, culture, and philosophy entirely foreign to contemporary believers. The pertinent questions of fourth- and fifth-century Christians are not ours today. According to Hellwig, people today are concerned with the meaning of Jesus in relationship to political, economic, racial and psychological freedom, as well as in relationship to extra-Christian religious traditions. Ultimately, she insists that while Chalcedon remains a pertinent source for any contemporary christological formulation, the meaning of Jesus cannot be found by beginning there:

> It [Chalcedon] is not, and has never been, the primary source for Christology. The primary source for Christology is the historical and risen Jesus as experienced and testified by the community of believers from the beginning. And the solution to the apparent dilemma is in the constant return to the source, through the sources.[56]

Chalcedon, significant as it is for Hellwig, is only one of those sources.

Hellwig and Ruether have a deep soteriological concern in common: What does it mean to claim that Jesus is Savior when the world in which we live is racked with injustice and oppression of every kind? But with regard to classical christology, their approaches are quite different.

As mentioned above, Hellwig insists that for the sake of the faithful, contemporary christological formulations cannot bypass Chalcedon because it represents a history of faith and doctrine that cannot be discarded. Ruether, on the other hand, argues that Chalcedon does not represent the message and praxis of the historical Jesus as we have it in the gospels, and consequently, that Chalcedon was a distortion in the development of christology.

Pastorally speaking, both have a point. Believers today, especially women, need to be affirmed in their refusal to accept traditional or contemporary christological formulations that dehumanize anyone because of gender, race or religion. Simultaneously, when correctly interpreted, Chalcedon *can be* appreciated as an authentic expression of faith in Jesus as the Christ. However, both agree that the starting point for christology is and must remain the historical Jesus as we know him through the gospels and testimony of the earliest Christian communities.

Also, Ruether would agree with Hellwig that Chalcedon's use of Greek philosophical concepts and categories, its language, symbolism, and imagery, reflect a worldview relevant to the people of that particular historical context. Both would agree that the continued use of that language, symbolism and imagery (given its ahistorical, philosophical, and cosmological character) is not helpful today. Ruether maintains that this resulted in a christological tradition that was used to justify and sanctify established hierarchies of race, sex, and class, thereby desecrating the message and praxis of the historical Jesus.

In addition, Ruether would agree with Hellwig regarding the negative social implications conveyed by the Chalcedonian formulation. She would, however, also urge Hellwig to take that critique further and apply it to the lives of those who have suffered, and continue to suffer from the "passivity" foisted upon them by the religious elite who benefit from their passivity.

Finally, both theologians recognize that the significant questions for people today differ widely from those of fourth- and fifth-century Christians, but they do not always agree on what these questions are. Specifically, Hellwig does not raise the question of sexism with regard to the tradition and Ruether does not raise the question of fidelity to the teaching of Chalcedon. Perhaps the most valuable lesson Hellwig and Ruether can teach us regarding christology and the tradition is that it is important not to stop questioning.

## Questions for Reflection and Discussion

1. Describe your own christological perspective with regard to Judaism. Are you more aligned with Ruether or Hellwig on this issue? Explain.

2. Can you support Paul Knitter's proposal for a liberation theology of the religions, especially as applied to the uniqueness of Jesus? Why or why not?

3. Ruether insists that interreligious dialogue must include women's experience of suffering and dialogue between feminists in both

historical and pagan religious traditions. Why does she take this position?

4. Given Monika Hellwig's silence with regard to feminism and christology, can one embrace a feminist christology and still be an "ecclesial" person?

5. How can the connections both Ruether and Thompson make between christology and ecology (using Jesus' ethics of self-limitation, conversion and the lordship of Christ as servanthood) challenge Christians socially, politically and spiritually?

6. Discuss what practical meaning the Chalcedonian definition of Jesus Christ as truly human and truly divine has had in your life. Where does this place you in relation to Ruether or Hellwig on the issue of christology and the tradition?

# ℊ CHAPTER 5

# Some Implications
# of Ruether's Christology

The purpose of this chapter is to suggest some implications of Ruether's christological perspective for methodology, anthropology, soteriology, ecclesiology, ecumenism, and spirituality. The Epilogue will indicate some limitations and raises further questions in terms of her contribution to current christological debates.

## Methodology

Method is of paramount importance in the contemporary christological debate. How one *does* christology reveals one's allegiances, values, politics, and vision, for all christological methods are biased. There is no such thing as "neutral" or "value-free" christology, since one's christology is a deeply personal faith response. Moreover, what is at stake in the method is not merely abstract truth, but the concrete lives, aspirations and hopes of many people, Christians and those of extra-Christian religious traditions alike, especially those who have been or are victimized by sexist, racist, classist, or imperialistic christological formulations. It is these people, as we have seen, who have shaped Ruether's christological perspective. Her christology suggests several implications for method.

  1) Christology should be done with profound attention to the

experience of those who have suffered under oppressive christo-logical formulations. For Ruether this means primarily women, along with people of color, Third World people, and people who are members of extra-Christian religious traditions, especially the Jews. Thus the method should reflect both "conscious partiali-ty" and a "view from below."[1]

2) Method in christology must be rooted in the message and prax-is of the historical Jesus who embodied the prophetic-messianic tradition. This implies recognizing Jesus as liberator of the poor and oppressed, who fought against the religious and political elite of his own day for lording their wealth and power over those most vulnerable. A method rooted in the message and praxis of the his-torical Jesus also includes making Jesus' vision of the Kingdom cen-tral to its work, a vision that began in this world in every effort to transform exploitative social structures and relationships.

3) Praxis must be integral to the way christology is done today; it must be the test of any theoretical assumption about Christ. As Ruether has so firmly stated, "...if the paradigms of christology perpetuate political detachment, religious bigotry, sexism and the negation of nature, then we have to ask serious questions about the saving content of Christology."[2] The truth of any christologi-cal statement can only be known in the ethical deeds to which it gives birth.

4) Christological method should be dialectical rather than dua-listic. A dialectical methodology both denounces and announces, both negates and affirms. It avoids the simplistic categorization of dualistic or oppositional thinking that heretofore has pitted men against women, soul against body, humankind against nature, Ro-man Catholics against Protestants, and Christians against members of other faith traditions. Because it is both critical and reconstruc-tive, dialectical method can provide a more holistic and integrated approach to human experience, Scripture and the tradition. Be-cause it invites an ethical critique of every christological formula, it enables us to construct an understanding of Jesus that is genuinely faithful to his message, praxis and vision of the Kingdom.

5) Ruether's christological perspective implies attention to the "underside" of the tradition, meaning, for example, previously con-demned or neglected alternatives to the dominant tradition such as the Wisdom tradition, spirit, and androgynous christologies. [3]

6) Method in christology should explore new models of Christ

that transcend and enlarge those of the past. These models should develop out of authentic interreligious dialogue, from the experience of women of color, poor women, and sexually abused women.

7) Method in christology should critique the humanocentrism that denigrates the covenantal harmony God intended for all creation.

8) Ruether's christological perspective implies that any method in christology should be done with a "hermeneutic of suspicion" regarding Scripture, tradition, and contemporary human experience. Too often methods in christology have reflected chauvinism, whether according to gender, race, religion, or geography.

## Anthropology

Ruether's christology is based on the message and praxis of the historical Jesus, who is, in her view, the liberator of the oppressed, one who sought to model relationships characterized by mutuality, compassion, and justice, rather than dominance and subservience. Further, Jesus was, for Ruether, the iconoclastic prophet whose words and deeds were the antithesis of those who used power and privilege to justify themselves at the expense of the marginalized in society. He was particularly sensitive to oppressed women and on many occasions repudiated the social and religious patriarchal mores of his day in order to heal, teach, and empower women, particularly poor women. He represented a new kind of humanity, best expressed not in his maleness, but in his message and ministry of good news to the poor.

Consequently, Ruether's christology requires that "an androcentric anthropology," which affirms the subordinate or auxiliary status of the female in relation to the male, be rejected.[4] This means a rejection of the patriarchal anthropology that has permeated classical Christian theology from ancient times to the present. Thus, her christological perspective requires denouncing the position that women represent the "lower" physical and sexual human nature vis-a-vis men who represent a higher, spiritual, and rational human nature; that women, inferior by nature, are more prone to sin, responsible for the Fall, and are therefore to be subjugated to men; and that women, because of their inferior nature and inclination to sin, cannot fully image God.

By way of contrast, Ruether's christology encourages the development of an egalitarian anthropology, one that recognizes the full personhood of women, affirm them as equally "theomorphic" (revealing God) and jointly responsible with men for the care of the created world. Her christology recognizes that God is to be imaged as both male and female without subordinating the female symbols to the male.[5] Further, because Ruether's christological perspective recognizes the incarnation to be inclusive of both genders, all races and historical conditions, it challenges Christian anthropology likewise to be inclusive. Non-androcentric insights found in the anthropologies of extra-Christian religious traditions and cultures beyond the Western hemisphere could be a rich resource for a deepened grasp of what it means to be a human being, both male and female.

Likewise, because her christology sees the past historical Jesus as *one* paradigm of redemptive humanity, it challenges believers to be open to other models, "particularly those that disclose the journey to redemptive personhood from women's experience."[6] Because her christology celebrates the humanity and full personhood of women, it invites us not only to an expanded understanding of what it means to be human, but also to a more inclusive understanding of the meaning of Christ. Christian anthropology could be truly transformed if it were open to the critical and liberating insights of Ruether's christology.

## Soteriology

A poignant and critical issue implied in Ruether's christology is undoubtedly soteriology: How does Jesus save? Given the sin, the "broken relationality," that pervades our world today, it is a question that must be confronted.

The historical Jesus, "as the particular and paradigmatic expression of God's Logos-Sophia for the Christian church," is the presence of God among us. As such, he is also "the symbol that embraces the authentic humanity and fulfilled hopes of all persons."[7] As a paradigm of liberated and redeemed humanity, Jesus reveals God to us as "Liberator," "Holy Wisdom," "Abba," "Christa"—a God intimately concerned about the welfare of all human beings and the entire universe.

The "God-consciousness" of Jesus, which flowed from his deep and abiding relationship with the divine, impelled him to pro-claim "a prophetic vision that stands in judgment on social and religious systems that exclude subordinated and marginated peo-ple from divine favor."[8] Thus, he denounced the oppressive struc-tures that kept the powerless of society in bondage to the power-ful. In addition, he announced the Kingdom, a new vision of justice, equality and peace where the poor would rejoice, cap-tives be freed, the blind given sight and prisoners freed. Hence, he offered hope of redemption to all who would repent of their hardness of heart and be open to one another as brothers and sis-ters. Significantly, this hope was a grace available to all; it was not based on gender, ethnic origin, education, wealth, or re-ligious affiliation.[9]

According to Ruether, the historical Jesus announced in his mes-sage and praxis "...not himself, but the liberated humanity to come."[10] And this is how he saves us. As a paradigm of liberated humanity, he models what it means to be authentically human. In his words and deeds he teaches us how to relate to one another, particularly to the poor and oppressed. As the model of redeemed humanity, he saves us from our sinful inclinations to distorted re-lationality, and points us toward our authentic potential as hu-man beings—the potential we all have to live in mutual and rev-erent relationship with one another and the earth. Further, he saves us by challenging us to *save one another in his name*, that is, to continue his task and mission of making the Kingdom come more concretely on this earth.

> This means that we, the Church, who know Christ no longer after the flesh but after the Spirit, carry on his presence in our midst, not by imitating any of his particu-larities of race or gender, but rather by preaching his word and living it in our lives. We must live as those who preach good news to the poor and repent of our false privi-leges of gender, race, class or culture.[11]

Consequently, the community of Christ must continue this pro-phetic denunciation and annunciation and make every effort to model our lives after the redemptive vision of Jesus. We must be willing to encounter Christ not only in the past historical Jesus, but in our *sisters* and brothers as well. Only then can the life, death, and resurrection of Jesus continue to have salvific significance in our deeply divided world. Only then can the Kingdom continue to come.

## Ecclesiology

A christological perspective that celebrates Jesus' deep respect for women has profound implications for a new ecclesiology. Such a christology demands:

1) That the church openly and fully acknowledge and repent of its long, sinful history of sexism toward women.

2) That the church change the attitudes and structures in its own institutions that keep women in subordinate and inferior positions. Specifically, this means that the church ordain women. It also means that the church must re-examine its stance on sex and sexuality, insofar as it victimizes women by making them suffer unnecessarily (particularly in regard to reproductive rights, divorce, and lesbianism).

3) That the church re-examine its understanding of the nuclear family and in doing so acknowledge the patriarchal and hierarchical oppression that is so often perpetuated in this structure.

4) That the church recognize that its call to obedience has often been a means of manipulation and control not only over women's choices, lives, and destinies, but even over their self-understanding. On the basis of this recognition, the church must revise the priority that obedience has had in teaching and praxis.

5) That the church affirm the moral agency and integrity of women and thereby acknowledge that women's lives and experience have been an unrecognized locus for the presence of the divine.

Ruether has suggested a means for accomplishing these ecclesiological transformations. It involves the question of responsible membership in both church and society. With regard to participation in the Roman Catholic church, she has urged that "critical minorities" concerned with intellectual freedom and social justice not abandon the institutional church. Instead, they should make use of the existing vehicles of spiritual community and ministry and reappropriate the ministry of Word, sacrament, and service dominated up to now by an ecclesiastical ruling class.[12] This reappropriation of spiritual power will result in new forms of community and ministry *within* the present institutional structure. In her words:

Once we have reappropriated our own spiritual power,

> then we can begin forming base communities for worship, consciousness-raising and mutual support; peace and justice centers to express our praxis in society; study groups to develop our theology; new noncanonical religious orders that can covenant to serve the poor, and so forth....We have to get beyond the position of emptiness, frustration, anger, loneliness and mental and spiritual exhaustion that comes from the struggle with unresponsive institutional structures. Only then, with a secure base of support for our own personal spiritual life, will we be liberated enough to address with maturity, objectivity and compassion, the problems of reforming this ancient juggernaut called the Roman Catholic Church.[13]

What Ruether is suggesting to "critical minorities" in the Roman Catholic church is certainly applicable to other religious denominations. Indeed, what she suggests is a "hard saying," not "cheap grace." It presupposes a basic commitment to community and to the need for ongoing conversion. It also requires an accountability to the larger community from those within the ranks of the "critical minorities," whose educational privileges, experience in community, and opportunities for consciousness-raising have been far more "liberating" than people whose experience of "church" is confined to the local parish. Consequently, Ruether sees church reform as a dialectical process in which small groups gather in the Spirit to articulate creative new visions and needs within the framework of the institutional church. These new movements become part of the historical life of the institution, and the institution, in turn, is given new life and vision through their impact upon it.[14]

One incarnation of this vision is the Women-Church movement which, according to Ruether, represents a new vision of church coming to birth through the union of Christianity and feminism. As an ecumenical movement, it seeks to develop a vision of the church "as an exodus community from patriarchy."[15]

> Women-Church means neither leaving the church as a sectarian group, nor continuing to fit into it on its terms. It means establishing bases for a feminist critical culture and celebrational community that have some autonomy from the established institutions. It also means sharing this critical culture and sense of community with many women

who are working within existing churches but who gather, on an occasional or regular basis, to experience the feminist vision that is ever being dimmed and limited by the parameters of the male-dominated institution. It means some women might worship only in alternative feminist liturgies; others might do so on a regular basis, while continuing to attend liturgies in traditional parishes into which they seek to inject something of this alternative; and some women might enter into these experiences only occasionally, such as at annual gatherings of women pastors or feminist retreats, where women worship and celebrate their community together in the context of these occasional communities.[16]

The Women-Church movement is an example of the dialectical process of church reform presently happening within the institutional church. It is a sign of hope and an experience of liberation for many women who would otherwise leave the institutional church. As Ruether has so provocatively remarked, "The Spirit is not confined to past institutions and their texts. It leads us into new futures. We don't know the path, for we make the path as we go...."[17] It is on such paths that women continue to model and live the Christic community to which Jesus' message, praxis and vision calls them.

As a liberation community, Women-Church recognizes its need for ongoing conversion and challenges the institutional church to do the same. Together both must realize their common mission to society—a mission based on Jesus' vision of the Kingdom.

Commitment to this mission, to building the Kingdom on earth, is another implication of Ruether's christology for ecclesiology. The mission of the church in society is rooted in the prophetic-messianic vision that seeks to transform the prevailing structures of exploitation and alienation. The mission recognizes that relationality and the building of community are central to discipleship. This presupposes the eradication of all relationships, both personal and social, built around hierarchy, patriarchy, or exploitation of any kind. It challenges Christians to be inclusive through relationships with both genders, all races and religions. It invites them to participate in the building of a Christian community by embodying Jesus' model of redemptive humanity in our relationships with one another. Thus, Jesus' vision of the Kingdom, carried on in the mission of the Christic community, seeks both a new humanity and a new society where the equality of all persons is affirmed; where both women and men democratically participate in the political process, employment and education; where all classist, racist, sexist, and imperialistic hierarchies are dismantled; where production and consumption needs exist in harmony with nature; where both women and men share child-raising, homemaking, creative activity, and decision making of every kind.[18] Such a society, modeled on Jesus as the paradigm of liberated humanity, will sustain and renew just and mutual relationships. It will, indeed, give witness to a redemptive way of life.

## Ecumenism

In 1965, Ruether wrote:

> I cannot play the "Catholic representative" in the Protestant world, because I no longer think of Protestants as "them," but rather as another aspect of the Catholic "we." I have, in this sense, moved beyond dialogue into something which might be called "intentional unity," into a catholicity which takes its "tradition" as the whole Christian experience, perhaps even the whole human experience, that catholicity as well-expressed by the poet Terrence: *homo sum et nihil humani a me alienum puto.* Such an attitude will be dubbed "fuzzy eclecticism" by many, but I would not consider it so. I feel it is a broadening of one's base of thinking which both enriches and clarifies the perception of truth.[19]

Almost 25 years later, her christological perspective testifies to this abiding view of Christianity, Catholicism, and religious truth. Its implications for ecumenism are several:

1) Without equivocation, Ruether's christology challenges the male-dominated ecumenical movement to take the oppression of women seriously. Further, it calls upon the movement to extirpate from all christological perspectives, whether Evangelical, mainline Protestant, or Roman Catholic, any and every understanding of Christ that denigrates the full personhood of women.[20]

2) She challenges Christians to understand the historical Jesus as the liberator of the poor and oppressed. Christians are called to

come together in solidarity with the marginalized and abused of the world over against the principalities and powers. Succinctly, Ruether's christology requires ecumenical Christianity to be a "justice church," clear in its repudiation of sexism, racism, classism, and imperialism. This is both a local and global challenge in the spirit of the prophetic dialectic, for as Ruether has candidly stated:

> When we open our hearts to all persons as bearers of God's image, we must also be prepared to incur the hostility of those social systems of this world, including those who call themselves "church," who are committed to the opposite view.[21]

Ruether's christology insists that Christians be inclusive and, in the spirit of Jesus, embrace the consequences.

3) Ruether calls Christians to see Christ at the "lead edge" of history rather than its center. Such a position can overcome the intolerance, bigotry and attitude of superiority that have marred Christian history by disclaiming any monopoly on divine revelation in Christ. Particularly, such a stance would improve Jewish-Christian relations and open the door for better dialogue with Hindus, Buddhists, Muslims and others. It can provide the opportunity for what Paul Knitter refers to as a new understanding of Christ as "one among many" in a relationship of "complementary uniqueness" with other salvific figures. Understanding Christ this way will also challenge Christians to recognize the need for ongoing personal and social conversion in any attempt to live an authentic Christian life. It can enable Christians to recognize that membership in the Christic community requires active participation in the building of the Kingdom on earth through the transformation of unjust social structures.

4) Ruether demands that we refuse to see the Jesus of the past as the only model of Christ. Because Ruether's christology not only reaffirms the tradition of God's incomprehensibility but also discovers the divine in "new" places (in women's experience, in extra-Christian religious traditions, etc.), it invites Christians to be open to "other" models of Christ, "other" paradigms of redeemed humanity. Hence, her christology encourages ecumenism to further dialogue regarding a non-normative, soteriocentric christology, as proposed by Paul Knitter.[22]

These suggestions do not exhaust the implications of Ruether's christology for ecumenism. Nevertheless, they demand that Christians rethink the meaning of the essential symbol of their faith. In fact, Ruether envisions this challenge as a community vocation:

> To be more fully alive, aware and committed, this is surely the meaning of a journey in faith. But this must mean that we are always reassessing and reappropriating the past—our own past experiences and reflections—in the light of new challenges.[23]

Hence, her christological perspective invites the ecumenical movement to be more fully alive, and to pursue this journey in a world marked by immense human suffering and religious pluralism. In light of her christology, then, I suggest that the challenge to the ecumenical movement is *kairos*.[24]

## Spirituality

I understand spirituality to mean, most fundamentally, relationship, the way one lives one's life in relationship to God, self, others, and the world. Ruether's theological stance requires a similar understanding of spirituality, one in which our relationships, both personal and social, comprise the constitutive dimension of our spirituality. With this in mind, there are several implications in her christology for spirituality.

1) The first of these implications lies in her very profound and inclusive view of the divine.

> By "God" I mean the transcendent matrix of Being that underlies and supports both our own existence and our continual potential for new being. This relation to God provides humanity with its authentic ground and potential (*imago dei*) over against the historical deformation of that potential by egoism, fear and self-alienation which give rise to systemic structures of social alienation and oppression: sexism, racism, classism and so on.[25]

To recognize God in this way enables one to understand Jesus in Ruether's terms: as paradigmatic of liberated humanity. Likewise, to recognize Jesus as paradigmatic of liberated humanity enables one to rethink and experience God anew and to recognize that this is the God Jesus points to.

Such a God is not confined to white, male Christians, but rather is revealed in both genders, all social classes and cultures. This is the God of Jesus Ruether has referred to as "the God of the Exodus," "Liberator," "Holy Wisdom," who "...leads us to the converted center, the harmonization of self and body, self and other, self and world. She/he is the *shalom* of our being."[26]

In Ruether's scheme, this is the God who is revealed in the ministry and message of Jesus as good news to the poor, the outcast, the unlovable. This is the God who, revealed in Jesus, protests against unjust social structures that perpetuate sexism, racism, classism, and imperialism. This is the God who, revealed in Jesus, calls us to relationships of mutuality and justice. This is the God who, revealed in Jesus, is a God of history, seeking to free us from slavery and lead us to the promised land of future wholeness and harmony.

For Ruether, such a God is not confined to a past historical model of Christ, but instead continues to be revealed in myriad historical circumstances and religious contexts. Such a God continues to be revealed in "other Christs," particularly the "Christa," or crucified woman.

To know Jesus as the paradigm of liberated humanity, as vindicator of the poor and oppressed, as one model of the Christ, is to know a God not confined to Jesus, but certainly defined in Jesus.[27] To know the divine as such is to recognize that the community of Christ must carry on Jesus' prophetic denunciations and annunciations of oppressive structures and attempt to model, in our own lives, the liberated humanity yet to come.[28] Maybe then we will begin "... to see the dynamic relationship between God as the source of our being and God as the empowerer of our aspirations and growth toward new being, toward redeemed and fulfilled humanity."[29]

2) Another implication of Ruether's christology for spirituality has to do with an understanding of the self in relation to others. To perceive Jesus, in her terms, as "an exponent of God's Word in his critique of oppressive structures and in his announcement of the Kingdom"[30] is to recognize the inestimable value relationality played in the life and vision of Jesus. As she has expressed it:

> Christology is that symbol of Christian theology that should manifest the face of God/ess as liberator. Christology should be filled with our best visions of the good potential of humans and the world concretely revealed. The

Savior figure brings together the human and the divine, disclosing at one and the same time, the gracious redeeming face of God/ess and our authentic potential.[31]

Jesus exemplified what it means to be truly human. His relationships were based, not on a hierarchy of sex, race, or class, but rather on mutuality and profound respect. Ruether asserts that no person was ever dehumanized by Jesus, that he actively sought on the contrary to lift up those most commonly demeaned by society in his day: women, prostitutes, tax collectors, Samaritans.

3) Ruether's christology implies that Christian spirituality recognize sin both as "broken or distorted" relationality, and as the need for ongoing conversion to the humanity of Jesus lived out in the body of Christ.

Ruether sees sin, in its most fundamental expression, as a distortion of the I-Thou relation between men and women in human community. This alienation is reflected in every dimension: "...from one's self as body, from the other as different from oneself, from nonhuman nature and from God/ess."[32] While she certainly acknowledges that sin is personal, she insists that it is also social. Clarifying this, Ruether has argued that sin "...is never just 'individual'; there is no evil that is not relational. Sin exists precisely in the distortion of relationality, including relation to oneself."[33] Speaking specifically about social sin, she has stated:

Social sin is...fundamentally culpable. However, our moral traditions of individual "sins" do not give us a good handle for analyzing the nature of culpability for social sin. Social sin continues across generations. It is historically inherited. Individuals are socialized into roles of domination and oppression and taught that these are normal and right. Discovery that the social system of which you are a part is engaged in chronic duplicity and contradiction, then, comes as a shock and an awakening. One has to reevaluate not only the social system but one's own life in it; not only what you have actually "done," but even more what you have accepted from it.[34]

Thus, social sin is the systemic embodiment of distorted relationality that issues from personal sin. Because it is built into social structures and institutions, it takes on a life of its own, aside from individual egoism, passivity and self-centeredness.

Conversion to community or to relationality is the response to both personal and social sin implied in Ruether's christology. It is a change of heart so deep that the values and vision of Jesus become the center of one's life and community. Conversion from sexism, racism, classism, and humanocentrism demands that we begin to model in our social relationships the new world we seek. It demands a new interiority and participation in a process whereby "the liberated self and the transformation of social systems are interconnected."[35] This perspective of conversion issues from Ruether's christological vision that understands Christ as:

> ...the mandate for redeemed humanity, crucified in history, resurrected in hope, going ever ahead of us to lead us to new understandings of God's will and our calling. Christ is our unrealized future - female and male; Black and White; even Christian and non-Christian. Redeemed humanity is not a captive of the Christian religion any more than it is of white or male dominance.[36]

This christological vision challenges Christians to deepen their understanding of sin and the need for conversion. It urges them to seek a new humanity and a new community based on Jesus' vision of the Kingdom, whose hallmark was just and mutual relationships with self, others, God, and the created world.

## Questions for Reflection and Discussion

1. Do you agree or disagree that one's christology is never "neutral" or "value-free"? Explain.

2. What are the implications of the claim that Jesus saves us "...by challenging us to *save one another in his name*"?

3. Discuss some of the issues confronting the Women-Church movement.

4. Ruether maintains that God continues to be revealed in "other Christs," especially crucified women. What is your reaction to this?

5. In the final analysis, what contribution does Ruether's christological perspective make toward diminishing global suffering and promoting interreligious dialogue in our world today?

# Epilogue

Ruether is the first Christian feminist to attempt a feminist christology. In this task she represents the broad array of issues and concerns that have informed North American feminism. The breadth of her view and its revolutionary character reflect her profound grasp of these issues and concerns, and simultaneously place limits on her yet uncompleted christological enterprise. Her christology must be seen as suggestive rather than definitive.

Being the first to do christology from a feminist perspective, Ruether labored under a dearth of material, which necessitated rethinking the sources for herself. The feminist material available was as fledgling as her own. Where this is most evident is in Ruether's presentation of the historical Jesus. This is a highly controversial subject even in New Testament studies of the most traditional kind. Many questions still remain about method and results.

In addition, the first major feminist analysis of the New Testament was not published until 1983, and represents a heuristic rather than definitive contribution.[1] Also, this publication's treatment of Jesus is its most controversial section. Ruether's fundamental insight, however, that Jesus sided first with the poor and oppressed, has been affirmed not only by Elisabeth Shüssler Fiorenza, but also by a basic consensus of New Testament scholarship. While there is little likelihood that Ruether's insight will be overturned, details pertinent to a clearer understanding of the historical Jesus remain to be uncovered and rethought as progress continues in feminist approaches to the New Testament.

Another limitation in the area of scriptural studies is Ruether's use of the Wisdom tradition. Although she suggests this tradition can be an alternative resource for a non-patriarchal christology, she does not develop her sources fully enough and thereby fails to construct an adequate picture of how this tradition can inform a feminist christology. Elizabeth Johnson has produced several scholarly articles that build in this direction.

Ruether's strength lies in her ability to paint the broad picture, to offer us a critical overview of a wide range of historical circumstances and cultural contexts. In doing so she provides us with a lens through which we can recognize the impact circumstances and contexts have had, and continue to have, on the voiceless and marginalized. While she has been faulted for "oversimplifying historical reality," she has succeeded in helping us understand the broad sweep of Western civilization from the "underside," from the perspective of those who have been its victims.[2] Her christological vision may at times lack clarity and precision but it remains essentially liberating and redemptive for women, the poor, people of color, and members of extra-Christian religious traditions. They shall be its final judge.

Ruether's work has not answered all the questions of how ethics and experience must transform christology. Can Christians continue to profess that Jesus Christ is savior and that the salvation he wrought gives meaning to human existence if this belief does little to change the meaninglessness of human existence experienced by so many in our world?[3] As believers in the salvific message and deeds of Jesus Christ, what are we to *do* when countless women, men and children remain hungry and imprisoned, unclothed and without shelter, strangers and unwelcomed among us? In light of religious pluralism, can we continue to make exclusive or inclusive salvation claims for Jesus Christ? With Carter Heyward we can ask "...is the most accurate barometer of a white Christian theologian's openness to solidarity...her/his christology?"[4] Is it necessary to disregard classical christology, or, at least to critique it, because it has seriously distorted Christian understanding of Jesus as savior? Ruether's christological critique and alternative proposal challenge us to confront these questions in light of their ethical and soteriological implications.

Ruether's passion is to relate theological theory to social praxis. This, in itself, is an important contribution to contemporary christological discussions. Her critique and proposal call attention to the fact that many people have been victimized by sexist, racist, and imperialistic christological formulations. Naming such suffering is the first step in rectifying it. Thus this work has sought to make it very clear that there is an undeniable connection between what we believe about Jesus as the Christ and what we do to one another in light of that belief. In addition, I have sought to examine these issues from a critical perspective by locating Ruether's christology within a larger North American context of contemporary christological concerns.

Finally, this book is a contribution to the ongoing development of feminist theology. By offering a serious reflection on Ruether's christological critique and alternative proposal, it calls attention to both the suffering and hope that characterize the lives of women of faith in the Christian tradition. In this sense Ruether's christology reminds us indeed that there is "a time to mourn and a time to dance."

Many may consider Ruether to be too extreme in her critique, even unorthodox in her conclusions. Nonetheless, she challenges us to hear the cry of the victims, of those who have suffered most under oppressive christological formulations. Whether one agrees with Ruether or not, a study of her christology will generate further questions among all concerned about what difference Jesus makes in today's anguished world.

# Notes

## Preface

1. Personal correspondence from Rosemary Radford Ruether, November 1984.

2. Rosemary Radford Ruether, *To Change the World: Christology and Cultural Criticism* (London: SCM Press Ltd., 1981), 29.

3. Ruether describes "humanocentrism" as "…making humans the norm and 'crown' of creation in a way that diminishes other beings in the community of creation." See Rosemary Radford Ruether, "Feminist Interpretation: A Method of Correlation," in *Feminist Interpretation of the Bible*, ed. Letty Russell (Philadelphia: Westminster Press, 1985), 116.

## Introduction

1. Rosemary Radford Ruether, *Disputed Questions: On Being a Christian* (Nashville: Abingdon Press, 1982), 54.

## Chapter 1

1. Rosemary Radford Ruether, "Social Sin," *Commonweal* 108 (January 30, 1981): 47.

2. Ibid.

3. Ruether, *Disputed Questions*, 18-24. These pages give some of Ruether's own reflections on her family background.

4. Ibid., 110.

5. Betty Friedan, *The Feminine Mystique* (New York: Dell Publishing Company, 1963), 14.

6. Ruether, *Disputed Questions*, 21.

7. Ibid.

8. Ibid.

9. Ibid., 20.

10. Ruether, "Beginnings: An Intellectual Autobiography," in *Journeys: The Impact of Personal Experience on Religious Thought*, ed. Gregory Baum (New York: Paulist Press, 1975), 36.

11. Ruether, *Disputed Questions*, 36.

12. Ibid., 24.

13. Ibid., 111.

14. Ibid., 45.

15. Ibid.

16. Ruether, "Beginnings," 40.

17. Ruether, *Disputed Questions*, 17.

18. Ibid., 24.

19. Ruether, "Beginnings," 38.

20. Ibid., 40.

21. Ibid.

22. Ruether, *Disputed Questions*, 17.

22. Ibid., 27.

23. Ruether, "Social Sin," 47.

25. Ruether, *Disputed Questions*, 36.

26. Ibid., 37.

27. Ibid., 114.

28. Ibid., 115.

29. Ibid., 117.

30. Ruether, "Beginnings," 51. In another article she states, "In the late 1960s two things came along: the Second Vatican Council and the civil-rights movement. I was caught up in civil rights, and I worked down in Mississippi for a while. And suddenly I got political, after all those years of having been somewhere back in the 5th century." See Ruether, "Sex: Female; Religion: Catholic; Forecast: Fair." *U.S. Catholic* 50 (April 1985): 19.

31. Ruether, "Beginnings," 51. Timing has been significant in Ruether's development. She herself has said, "The 1960s occurred for me between the ages of 23 and 32. This means that a critical state of my adult identity coalesced both with the decade of Catholic renewal and the decade of American social crisis. If I had been born ten years earlier, I might well stand in a different place today." See Ruether, "Asking the Existential Questions," *The Christian Century* 97 (April 2, 1980): 376.

32. Ruether, *Disputed Questions*, 36-40.

33. Ruether, "Social Sin," 47.

34. Ruether, *Disputed Questions*, 76.

35. Ruether, "Beginnings," 53.

36. Ruether, "Social Sin," 47.

37. Ruether, *Disputed Questions*, 118.

38. Ibid., pp. 109-142. See also Ruether, *Sexism and God-Talk* (Boston: Boston Press, 1983), 201-266.

39. Ruether, "Beginnings," 53.

40. Ruether, *Disputed Questions*, 83.

41. Ruether, "Rich Nations/Poor Nations: Toward a Just World Order in the Era of Neo-Colonialism," in *Christian Spirituality in the United States: Independence and Interdependence*, ed. Francis A. Eigo (Villanova, Pennsylvania: Villanova University Press, 1978), 59.

42. Ruether, "Libertarianism and Neo-Colonialism: The Two Faces of America," *Christianity and Crisis* 36 (August 16, 1976): 181. See also, Ruether, "Rich Nations/Poor Nations," 59-63 and "Letter of Rosemary Ruether to Sergio Torres and the Planners of the Conference," in *Theology in the Americas* eds. Sergio Torres and John Eagleson (Maryknoll, New York: Orbis Books, 1976), 84-86.

43. Ruether, *Disputed Questions*, 91.

44. Ruether, *Disputed Questions*, 141. See also Ruether, "Asking the Existential Questions," 378.

45. Ruether, "Beginnings," 44. She does say that she read Marx as an undergraduate. See Ruether, *Disputed Questions*, 85.

46. Ruether, "Beginnings," 44.

47. Ruether, *Disputed Questions*, 141.

48. Ibid., 142.

49. Ibid.

50. With great clarity, Judith Vaughan has illustrated Ruether's dialectical methodology by contrasting it with an oppositional or dualistic approach. See her excellent study, *Sociality, Ethics and Social Change: A Critical Appraisal of Reinhold Niebuhr's Ethics in the Light of Rosemary Radford Ruether's Works* (Lanham: University of America Press, 1983).

51. Ruether, *Liberation Theology: Human Hope Confronts Christian History and American Power* (New York: Paulist Press, 1973), 182.

52. When using this term Ruether is calling for a new textual base for theology that issues from women's experience.

53. Ruether, "Asking the Existential Questions," 377. See also Ruether, "A Method of Correlation," for a further explanation of how she understands the prophetic-messianic tradition.

54. Ruether, "Messiah of Israel and the Cosmic Christ: A Study of the Development of Christology in Judaism and Early Christianity." Unpublished manuscript. Washington, D.C., 1971, 46-56. Ruether explains further that, "There has been much discussion among scholars about the

source of the 'prophetic pattern' of wrath and redemption, judgment and future hope that is characteristic of the prophets.... We are suggesting here that this 'prophetic pattern' is nothing else than the common oriental religious pattern of yearly distress and salvation, as this was interpreted existentially and anthropologically by the Hebrew temple cult and then interpreted in historical and ethical terms by the prophets." (Ibid., 46. ) With regard to this manuscript Ruether states: "...the original manuscript still lies in my drawer unpublished, although I constantly use pieces of it in teaching and writing. I am not sure whether I will ever go back and do the polishing necessary to publish this work, yet it lies behind much of my subsequent writing on Christian origins in Christology, anti-Semitism, the Goddess and Mariology, and, finally, on political theology." See Ruether, *Disputed Questions*, 51.

55. Ibid., 46-49. Ruether uses Amos 4:1-9; 12;5, 18-24, and Hosea 4:1-3 to illustrate this.

56. Ibid. See also Ruether, *Disputed Questions*, 34.

57. Ruether, "Messiah of Israel," 52.

58. Ruether, "Feminism and Patriarchal Religion: Principles of Ideological Critique of the Bible." *Journal for the Study of the Old Testament* 22 (1982): 60. See also Ruether, *Sexism and God-Talk: Toward a Feminist Theology,* (Boston: Beacon Press, 1983), 27-31.

59. Ruether, *Faith and Fratricide: The Theological Roots of Anti-Semitism* (New York: Seabury Press, 1979), 131.

60. Ruether, *Disputed Questions*, 32-33.

61. Ruether, "A New Political Consciousness," *The Ecumenist* 8 (May-June 1970): 61.

62. Ruether, *To Change the World*, 11.

63. Ibid., 14-17.

64. Ruether, *Faith and Fratricide*, 230.

65. Ruether, "Feminism and Religious Faith: Renewal or New Creation?," *Religion and Intellectual Life* 3 (Winter 1986): 10.

66. Ibid., 11.

67. Ibid.

68. Ibid., 12.

69. Ibid.

70. Ibid., 13.

71. Ibid.

72. Ibid., 14. See also Ruether, "A Method of Correlation," 111-124.

73. Ruether, "Feminism and Religious Faith," 14.

74. Ibid., 15. See Judith Plaskow, "The Coming of Lilith: Toward a Feminist Theology," in *Womanspirit Rising: A Feminist Reader in Religion*, eds. Carol P. Christ and Judith Plaskow (San Francisco: Harper & Row, 1979), 198-209.

75. Ruether, "Feminism and Religious Faith," 15.

76. Ibid., 15-16.

77. Ruether, "Feminist Theology in the Academy," *Christianity and Crisis* 45 (March 4, 1985): 61.

78. Ruether, "Feminism and Religious Faith," 16-17.

79. Ibid.

80. Ibid., 18.

81. Ibid., 18-19.

82. Ibid., 19-20.

83. Carol P. Christ is also very critical of Ruether's use of the prophetic-messianic tradition as the basis for a feminist methodology. See Carol P. Christ, *Laughter of Aphrodite: Reflections on a Journey to the Goddess* (San Francisco: Harper & Row, 1987), 57-71.

84. Elisabeth Schüssler Fiorenza, *In Memory of Her: A Feminist Theolgical Reconstruction of Christian Origins* (New York: Crossroad, 1983), 17-18.

85. Ruether, "Review Symposium: *In Memory of Her: A Feminist Theological Reconstruction of Christian Origins*," by Elisabeth Schussler Fiorenza. *Horizons* 11 (Spring 1984): 148.

86. Ibid.

87. These are very similar to the four basic themes Ruether refers to on p. 24 of *Sexism and God-Talk*. However, in the "Review Symposium," Ruether does reword and enlarge these. See p. 148.

88. Ibid., 148-149.

89. Ibid.

90. Ruether, "A Method of Correlation," 117.

91. Ibid., 118.

## Chapter 2

1. Ruether, ed. *Religion and Sexism: Images of Women in the Jewish and Christian Traditions* (New York: Simon & Schuster, 1974), and *Faith and Fratricide*, 1979.

2. Personal correspondence from Ruether, March 1985.

3. Ruether, "Feminist Theology in the Academy," 57.

4. Ruether, "Messiah of Israel," 62ff.

5. Ruether, To Change the World, 13.

6. Ruether, "Messiah of Israel," 54-62. See above 28-29.

7. Ibid., 62-78.

8. Ibid., 83-84.

9. Ibid., 84.

10. Ibid.

11. Ibid., 84-85.

12. Ibid.

13. Ibid., 90.

14. Ibid., 92, 95. Ruether has also written, "Moreover, Jesus preferred as his title for the coming One (who he did not identify with himself) the term "Son of Man." This term, drawn from the book of Daniel and other apocalyptic literature, makes the Messiah a collective expression of Israel who, in turn, represents generic humanity. Since generic humanity cannot today be seen as normatively male, the Inclusive Language Lectionary by the National Council of Churches in the United States has chosen to translate this messianic title used by Jesus as "the Human One." See Ruether, "The Liberation of Christology from Patriarchy," Religion and Intellectual Life 2 (Spring 1985): 120.

15. Ibid., 103.

16. Ibid., 101-105.

17. Ibid., 117.

18. Ibid.

19. Ruether, To Change the World, 13.

20. Ruether, "Messiah of Israel," 22-23.

21. Ibid., 38-39. See also, Ruether, To Change the World, 11-12.

22. Ruether, "Messiah of Israel," 43.

23. Ibid., 55.

24. Ibid.

25. Ibid., 56-57. See also, Zechariah 9:9-10, 17; 10:1; 14:3, 6-9, 16-19.

26. Ibid., 59-60.

27. Ibid., 82.

28. Ibid., 110.

29. Ibid., 111.

30. Ibid., 315.

31. Ibid., 163.

32. Ibid., 166.

33. Ibid., 166-167.

34. Ibid., 169-170.

35. Ibid., 173-174.

36. Ibid., 175.

37. Ibid., 178.

38. Ibid., 179.

39. Ibid., 180.

40. Ibid., 181ff.

41. Ibid., 194-195.

42. Ibid., 197.

43. Ibid.

44. Ruether, *Faith and Fratricide*, 69. See also, Ruether, "Messiah of Israel," 53-54.

45. Ruether, *Faith and Fratricide*, 66.

46. Ibid., 70.

47. Ibid., 64-65.

48. Ibid., 70f. See also Ruether, "Anti-Semitism in Christian Theology," *Theology Today* 30 (January 1974): 366.

49. Ibid., 369.

50. Ibid., 370.

51. Ibid., 371.

52. Ibid.

53. Ruether, *Faith and Fratricide*, Chapter 3. See also Ruether, "The *Adversus Judaeos* Tradition in the Church Fathers: The Exegesis of Christian Anti-Judaism," in *Aspects of Jewish Culture in the Middle Ages*, ed. Paul E. Szarmach (Albany: State University of New York Press, 1979), 27-50; Ruether, "Anti-Semitism in Christian Theology," 365-382; Ruether, *To Change the World*, 31-43.

54. Ruether, *Faith and Fratricide*, 124-164; "The Adversus Judaeos Tradition," 30-47; "Anti-Semitism in Christian Theology," 374-377.

55. Ibid., 228-232. See also Ruether, *To Change the World*, 33-37.

56. Ibid.

57. Ibid.

58. Ibid.

59. Ruether, *To Change the World*, 38.

60. Ibid., 39.

61. Ruether, *Faith and Fratricide*, 239.

62. Ruether, *To Change the World*, 39.

63. Ibid.

64. Ruether, *Faith and Fratricide*, 240.

65. Ruether, *Disputed Questions*, 66.

66. Ruether, *Faith and Fratricide*, 238.

67. Ibid. Also, in "Messiah of Israel" Ruether has elaborated on realized or fulfilled messianism: "The Christian must also see that there is an idolatrous side to a misappropriated idea of realized messianism which can lend a stamp of inerrancy and absolutism to ...human historical projects, and this kind of idolatry of realized messianism has been an important element in the Christian's evil history of imperialism and genocide against the Jew, the red, black and yellow [people] around the world." See, "Messiah of Israel," 426.

68. Ruether, "Theological Anti-Semitism in the New Testament," 194-196.

69. Ibid., 196.

70. Ibid.

71. Ruether, "Messiah of Israel," 425.

72. Ibid., 426-429.

73. Ibid., 430.

74. Ibid., 435.

75. Ibid., 436.

76. Ibid., 437.

77. Ruether, *Disputed Questions*, 72.

78. Ibid., 73. Elsewhere she has also stated, "My own assumption is that the Divine Being that generates, upholds, and renews the world is truly universal, and is the father and mother of all peoples without discrimination. This means that true revelation and true relationship to the divine is to be found in all religions. God/ess is the ground of all beings, and not just of human beings." See Ruether, "Feminism and Jewish-Christian Dialogue: Particularism and Universalism in the Search for Religious Truth," in *The Myth of Christian Uniqueness: Toward a Pluralistic Theology of Religions*, eds. John Hick and Paul F. Knitter (Maryknoll, New York: Orbis Books, 1987), 141.

79. Ruether's christological proposal regarding anti-Judaism can be found in her *Disputed Questions*, 71-73; *To Change the World*, 42-43, and *Faith and Fratricide*, 246-261.

## Chapter 3

1. Ruether, *Disputed Questions*, 92-93.

2. Ibid., 92.

3. Ruether has pointed out that Latin American liberation theology's use of the prophetic paradigm differs from the feminist use of it. "Latin American liberation theologians can imagine when they take a text [from the Scriptures] about the oppression of the poor that the word 'poor' in antiquity meant something similar to their critique of poverty in Latin America... Feminists can have no such illusions of liberal continuity... . Feminist hermeneutics thus claims the power to retell the story in new ways, a power which has not been owned by other liberation theologies." See Ruether, "Feminism and Religious Faith," 14.

4. Ruether, "Christology and Latin American Liberation Theology," in *To Change the World*, 20.

5. Ibid., 20-21.

6. Ibid., 14.

7. Ibid., 14-15.

8. Ibid., 16.

9. Ibid., 17.

10. Ibid., 21.

11. Ibid., 22.

12. Ibid., 23.

13. Ruether, "Rich Nations," 82.

14. Ibid., 83.

15. Ruether, *To Change the World*, 23.

16. Ibid.

17. Ibid., 26.

18. Ibid. More recently Ruether has stated, in response to the Vatican admonition against liberation theology, that "A church on the side of the powerful wishes to extend charity to the poor, but not to stand with them in a way that woud be in conflict with the interests of economic and military elites. This is the real meaning of the hostility of churchmen to "class analysis" and "class struggle," and not, as they would contend, their desire to spread "love" and acceptance around equally to all classes." See

Ruether, *Contemporary Roman Catholicism: Crisis and Challenges* (Kansas City, Mo.: Sheed & Ward, 1987)j: 61.

19. Ruether, *To Change the World*, 28-30.

20. Ibid., 28.

21. See José Míguez Bonino, ed., *Faces of Jesus: Latin American Christologies*, trans. Robert Barr (Maryknoll, New York: Orbis Books, 1984).

22. Ruether, *Disputed Questions*, 86-90. See also several sources that expose the limits of capitalism in this context, e.g. Ruether, "Rich Nations," *passim*; Lee Cormie, "The Sociology of National Development and Salvation History," in *Sociology and Human Destiny*, ed. Gregory Baum (New York: Seabury, 1980), 240-259; Teresa Hayter, *The Creation of World Poverty*, (London: Pluto Press, 1983); Gustavo Gutiérrez, *A Theology of Liberation*, (Maryknoll, New York: Orbis Books, 1973), 21-27; 82-88; Fernando Henrique Cardosa and Enzo Faletto, *Dependency and Development in Latin America*, trans. Marjory Mattingly Urquidi (Berkeley: University of California Press, 1979); Juan Luis Segundo, "Capitalism Versus Socialism: Crux Theologica," in *Frontiers of Theology in Latin America*, ed. Rosino Gibellini (Maryknoll, New York: Orbis Books, 1978), 240-259.

23. Ruether, "Rich Nations," 82.

24. See Ruether, "Ecology and Human Liberation: A Conflict Between the Theology of History and the Theology of Nature," in *To Change the World*, 57-70.

25. Ruether, *To Change the World*, 68.

26. Ibid., 69.

27. Ruether, *Womanguides; Readings Toward a Feminist Theology* (Boston: Beacon Press, 1985), 196-197.

28. Ruether, *Sexism and God-Talk*, 72-92.

29. Judith Vaughan, *Sociality, Ethics and Social Change*, 118-119.

30. Ruether, "Feminist Theology and Spirituality," in *Christian Feminism: Vision of a New Humanity*, ed. Judith Weidman (San Francisco: Harper & Row, 1984), 18.

31. Ibid., 18-19.

32. Ibid., 19.

33. Ibid., 20.

34. Ibid.

35. Ruether, *To Change the World*, 45.

36. Ruether, "Messiah of Israel," 173. See also Ruether, *Sexism and God-*

*Talk,* 122 and Ruether, "The Liberation of Christology from Patriarchy," *Religion and Intellectual Life* 2 (Spring 1985): 120.

37. Ruether, "Messiah of Israel," 314. See also 68-69 above.

38. Ibid.

39. Ibid.

40. Ibid., 317.

41. Ruether, *Womanguides,* 109.

42. Ibid.

43. Ibid.

44. Ibid. See also Ruether, "The Liberation of Christology from Patriarchy," 117-128.

45. Ruether, "The Liberation of Christology from Patriarchy." 116.

46. Ibid., 117.

47. Ruether, *To Change the World,* 48.

48. Ruether, *Sexism and God-Talk,* 123-124.

49. Ruether, "Augustine and Christian Political Theology," *Interpretation: A Journal of Bible and Theology* 29 (July 1975): 256-257.

50. Ruether, *To Change the World,* 48-49; *Sexism and God-Talk,* 122-125, and "The Liberation of Christology from Patriarchy," 122-125.

51. Ruether, "The Liberation of Christology from Patriarchy," 117-118.

52. Ruether, "Misogynism and Virginal Feminism in the Fathers of the Church," In *Religion and Sexism,* 156ff. See also Ruether, *Liberation Theology,* 99-102; *To Change the World,* 45; and "The Liberation of Christology from Patriarchy," 118.

53. Ruether, *Disputed Questions,* 120-121; *To Change the World,* 45; "The Liberation of Christology from Patriarchy," 118-119, and *Sexism and God-Talk,* 97-99.

54. Ruether, "The Liberation of Christology from Patriarchy," 120.

55. Ibid.

56. For a careful study of the influence of the Wisdom tradition on christology see Elizabeth A. Johnson, "Jesus, the Wisdom of God: A Biblical Basis for a Non-Androcentric Christology," in *Ephemerides Theologicae Lovanienses* 61 (December 1985): 291.

57. Ruether, *Sexism and God-Talk,* 127-130; *To Change the World,* 49-53; and "The Liberation of Christology from Patriarchy," 125.

58. Ruether, *Sexism and God-Talk,* 130.

59. Montanism was a charismatic movement that arose in the middle of

the second century. It threatened the emerging understanding of Christianity as an episcopal hierarchy. It also numbered among its beliefs the idea that women, as well as men, were given the gift of prophecy. See Ruether, *Women-Church: Theology and Practice of Feminist Liturgical Communities* (San Francisco: Harper & Row, 1985), 12-13.

60. Ruether, *Sexism and God-Talk*, 132-134 and "The Liberation of Christology from Patriarchy," 123-125.

61. Ibid., 124-126 and 132-134.

62. Ruether, *Sexism and God-Talk*, 135. For her reasons, see Ruether, *To Change the World*, 55, and Ruether, "Feminist Theology and Spirituality," 12-13.

63. Ruether, *Sexism and God-Talk*, 136-137. See also Ruether, "The Liberation of Christology from Patriarchy," 122, 127, Ruether, *Womanguides*, 108-109, and Ruether, *Womenchurch*, 33, 149.

64. Ruether, *Sexism and God-Talk*, 136-137.

65. Ruether, *To Change the World*, 54.

66. Ruether, *Sexism and God-Talk*, 137. See also Ruether, "The Liberation of Christology from Patriarchy," 127.

67. Ruether, *Sexism and God-Talk*, 137.

68. Ruether, "The Liberation of Christology from Patriarchy," 127.

69. Ruether, *Sexism and God-Talk*, 137-138.

70. Ibid., 138.

71. Ruether, *To Change the World*, 56. See also Ruether, "The Future of Feminist Theology in the Academy," *Journal of the American Academy of Religion* 53 (December 1985): 704, 711; Ruether, "Feminism and Religious Faith," 15-16; and, "The Liberation of Christology from Patriarchy," 128.

72. Carter Heyward, "An Unfinished Symphony of Liberation: The Radicalization of Christian Feminism Among White U.S. Women: A Review Essay," *Journal of Feminist Studies in Religion* 1 (Spring 1985): 100.

73. Ruether, "Rich Nations," 81.

74. See Chapter 2.

75. Ruether, "Messiah of Israel," 317; "Feminist Theology the Spirituality," 20-22; *Sexism and God-Talk*, 116-126 and 134-138. *Womanguides*, 105-113; "The Liberation of Christology from Patriarchy," and "Feminism and Jewish-Christian Dialogue," 137-142.

76. Ruether, "Feminist Theology and Spirituality," 20-22; *Womanguides*, 105-113; "The Liberation of Christology from Patriarchy," 117-128, and *Sexism and God-Talk*, 116-138.

77. Ruether, "Feminist Theology and Spirituality," 22.

78. Ruether, "Feminist Theology in the Academy," 61. See also Ruether, "The Future of Feminist Theology in the Academy," 710-711, and "Feminism and Religious Faith," 15-17.

79. Ruether, "Rich Nations," 81.

## Chapter 4

1. There are other North American Roman Catholic theologians belonging to this category, such as John Pawlikowski who has written extensively on Jewish-Christian relations. He also discusses and criticizes Ruether's contribution to this debate. See John T. Pawlikowski, *Christ in the Light of the Christian-Jewish Dialogue* (New York: Paulist Press, 1982). Recommended reading on this subject also includes John Hick and Paul F. Knitter, eds. *The Myth of Christian Uniqueness: Toward a Pluralistic Theology of Religions* (Maryknoll, New York: Orbis Books, 1987).

2. Ruether, *To Change the World*, 31. See also Ruether, *Faith and Fratricide*, 246.

3. Monika Hellwig, "From the Jesus of Story to the Christ of Dogma," in *Anti-Semitism and the Foundations of Christianity*, ed. Alan Davies (New York: Paulist Press, 1979), 118-136.

4. Ibid. See 133, n.1 and 119-120.

5. Ibid., 120-124.

6. Ibid., 127.

7. Ibid.

8. Ibid., 128.

9. Ibid., 127-128.

10. Ibid., 128-129.

11. Regarding the terms "exclusive" and "inclusive," Hellwig states: "It is exclusive if the Christian experience of reintegration and reconciliation is interpreted as qualitatively distinct and discontinuous with any and all other experiences." It is "inclusive" if Christians "...reflect upon the quality of the experience that leads to the message of salvation [and]...recognize that quality of experience. . .in others." Ibid., 129.

12. Ibid., 128-133.

13. Ruether, "The Faith and Fratricide Discussion: Old Problems and New Dimensions," in *AntiSemitism and the Foundations of Christianity*, ed. Alan Davies (New York: Paulist Press, 1979), 242-243.

14. Hellwig, *Jesus the Compassion of God* (Wilmington, Delaware: Michael Glazier, Inc., 1983), 133.

15. Ibid., 139.

16. Regarding the organization of her book, it is not until the third and final section of it, "The Believer's Christ in a Pluralistic World," that Hellwig discusses extra-Christian religious beliefs.

17. See Chapter 2.

18. Paul Knitter, *No Other Name?: A Critical Survey of Christian Attitudes Toward the Religions* (Maryknoll, New York: Orbis Books, 1985), 194. See also Matthew L. Lamb, *Solidarity With Victims: Toward a Theology of Social Transformation* (New York: Crossroad, 1982), 134-143.

19. See Chapter 3, 50-56.

20. Ruether, "Crises and Challenges of Catholicism Today," *America* 154 (March 1, 1986): 156.

21. According to Knitter, a theocentric model of christology is based on the relational uniqueness of Jesus. Such a model affirms that Jesus is unique, but this uniqueness is defined by its ability to include and be included by other unique religious figures. Thus, this understanding of Jesus sees him as neither exclusive nor normative, but rather, as theocentric, "as a universally relevant manifestation of divine revelation and salvation." See Knitter, *No Other Name?: A Critical Survey of Christian Attitudes Toward the World Religions* (Maryknoll, New York: Orbis Books, 1985), 171-172.

22. Knitter, "Review Symposium" *Horizons* 13 (Spring 1986): 134.

23. Knitter, "Toward a Liberation Theology of Religions" in *The Myth of Christian Uniqueness: Toward a Pluralistic Theology of Religions* eds. John Hick and Paul Knitter (Maryknoll, New York: Orbis Books, 1987), 187.

24. Ibid., 178.

25. A "hermeneutics of suspicion" is a basic methodological tool of liberation theology. It exposes how easily religious doctrine can be used ideologically i.e., to maintain the power and privilege of one group over another. For a clear explanation of this see Paul Lakeland, *Freedom in Christ: An Introduction to Political Theology* (New York: Fordham University Press, 1986), 49-67.

26. Ruether, "Feminism and Jewish-Christian Dialogue," 147.

27. Ibid.

28. Ibid.

29. Knitter, *No Other Name?*, 202.

30. Ruether, "Messiah of Israel," 437. See also Ruether, "In What Sense Can We Say That Jesus is the Christ?," *The Ecumenist* 10 (January-February, 1972): 22.

31. Here I am following Knitter's categories. "Exclusive uniqueness" means "...that only in Jesus can true revelation or salvation be found. In such an understanding the Christ event is *constitutive* of any true encounter with God, anywhere in history." "Inclusive uniqueness" means " ...God's revealing-saving action in Jesus includes all other religions, either as an anonymous, cosmic presence within them or as their final fulfillment. In this view, Jesus remains, if not constitutive of, *normative* for, all religious experience, for all times." See Knitter, *No Other Name?: A Critical Survey of Christian Attitudes Toward the Religions* (Maryknoll, New York: Orbis Books, 1985), 171.

32. My interpretation of Ruether on this issue is taken from the following sources: Ruether, *To Change the World*, 45-56; *Sexism and God-Talk*, 116-138; *Womanguides*, 105-113; "In What Sense Can We Say That Jesus is the Christ?," 22; "The Liberation of Christology from Patriarchy," 117-128; and personal correspondence from Ruether, March 1986.

33. Ruether, *Womanguides*, 112-113.

34. Knitter, "Toward a Liberation Theology of Religions," 191-192.

35. Ibid., 194.

36. Ibid., 195-196.

37. Ibid., 196.

38. Ruether, "The Liberation of Christology from Patriarchy," 127.

39. Ibid.

40. Ibid.

41. Ibid., 201-204. Here Knitter is referring to H. Richard Niebuhr's suggestion "...that Christians adopt a *confessional* approach to others—that is, that they confess and make known what they have experienced God to have done for them and the world in Jesus, *without* making any claims about Jesus' superiority or normativity over other religious figures." 203.

42. Ibid., 204.

43. Elizabeth A. Johnson, "Seminar on Christology," in *Proceedings of the Catholic Theological Society of America* 40 (1985): 186. The seminar discussed Hellwig's *Jesus the Compassion of God* and Ruether's *Sexism and God-Talk*. Johnson presented a brief summary of the discussion.

44. William M. Thompson, *The Jesus Debate: A Survey and Synthesis* (New York: Paulist Press, 1985), 201-202.

45. Ibid., 338. Similarly, Ruether talks about an "ecological ethic," though she does not connect it as explicitly with Jesus as Thompson does. See Ruether, *Sexism and God-Talk*, 91.

46. Thompson, *The Jesus Debate*, 292.

47. Ibid., 338-341.

48. Ruether, *Womanguides*, 108-109.

49. Thompson, *The Jesus Debate*, 421.

50. Ibid., 422.

51. Ibid., 341. Thompson has also spoken about conversion with regard to ecology by calling for "a heightened emphasis upon the sacramentality of nature." See William M. Thompson, "Dappled and Deep Down Things: A Meditation on Christian Ecological Trends" *Horizons* 14 (Spring 1987): 64-81.

52. I am using "tradition" in the way Thompson uses it, "...the so-called *tradita*: Scripture and nonscriptural traditions [prayer, liturgy, art, doctrine, Christian experiences in general, etc.]." See Thompson, *The Jesus Debate*, 52.

53. Hellwig, *Jesus the Compassion of God*, 33-61.

54. Ibid., 33-42.

55. Ibid., 36. See also Hellwig, "Christology and Attitudes towards Social Structures," in *Above Every Name: The Lordship of Christ and Social Systems*, ed. Thomas Clarke (New York: Paulist Press, 1980), 13-34.

56. Ibid., 42.

## Chapter 5

1. Elisabeth Schüssler Fiorenza, "On Feminist Methodology," *Journal of Feminist Studies in Religion* 1 (Fall 1985): 74-75.

2. Ruether, *To Change the World*, 4.

3. As church historian, Anne Llewellyn Barstow, has stated in this regard, "But herein lies the strength of women's history: it challenges the accepted norms of class, race, and religious identification of Western history, thus forcing the historian into interdisciplinary methodologies and a cross-cultural perspective. Because feminist scholars, in common with other minority-group scholars, must question the methods and values of every discipline, our political consciousness is sharpened and our own methodology is stretched." See Anne Llewellyn Barstow, "On Feminist Methodology," *Journal of Feminist Studies in Religion* 1 (Fall 1985): 88.

4. See Ruether, "Feminist Theology and Spirituality," 22-23 and "The Liberation of Christology from Patriarchy," 127.

5. Ruether, "The Liberation of Christology from Patriarchy," 126-127. See also Ruether, *Sexism and God-Talk*, 93-115.

6. Ruether, *Sexism and God-Talk*, 115.

7. Ruether, "The Liberation of Christology from Patriarchy," 116 and 127. See also 65-66 above.

8. Ibid., 120.

9. Ibid., 127.

10. Ruether, "Feminist Theology and Spirituality," 23.

11. Ruether, "The Liberation of Christology from Patriarchy," 128.

12. Ruether, "Crises and Challenges of Catholicism Today," *America* 154 (March 1, 1986): 157. Further clarifying her point on this issue she has stated: "Reappropriation theology means a basic spiritual revolution in our consciousness that puts our lives, as the community, at the center of the meaning of being church, rather than seeing ourselves at the periphery, banging on locked doors, ever asking for permission to breathe from those we imagine own the conduits of the Spirit." See Ruether, *Contemporary Roman Catholicism*, 67.

13. Ibid.

14. Ibid., 158.

15. Ruether, *Womanguides*, 161.

16. Ruether, *Women-Church: Theology and Practice* (San Francisco: Harper & Row, 1985), 62. Feminist biblical scholar Elisabeth Schussler Fiorenza has also written on the Women-Church movement: "In exorcising the internalized sin of sexism as well as in calling the whole Christian Church to conversion feminist theology reclaims women's Christian 'birthright' of being Church, fully gifted and responsible members of the 'body of Christ' who have the power to articulate our own theology, to reclaim our own spirituality, and to determine our own and our sisters' religious life. As women-church we celebrate our vision and power for change, we ritualize our struggles, we articulate our own theological insights, and share our strength by intellectually and spiritually nurturing each other." See Elisabeth Schüssler Fiorenza, "For Women in Men's Worlds: A Critical Feminist Theology of Liberation" in *Concilium* 171, *Different Theologies, Common Responsibility: Babel or Pentecost?* eds. Claude Geffre, Gustavo Gutierrez and Virgilio Elizondo (Edingburgh: T.& T. Clark, Ltd., 1984), 37. It is this article that led me to claim that Women-Church is an ecumenical movement. However, according to Mary Jo Weaver, it is a "...broadly inclusive movement [within the Roman Catholic church] that is expected to become ecumenical in the future." See Mary Jo Weaver, *New Catholic Women: A Contemporary Challenge to Traditional Religious Authority* (San Francisco: Harper & Row, 1985), 133.

17. Ruether, *Womanguides*, 248.

18. Ruether, "Feminist Theology and Spirituality," 26-27, 31.

19. Ruether, "Catholicism and Catholicity," in *The Generation of the Third Eye*, ed. Daniel Callahan (New York: Sheed & Ward, 1965), 191-192.

20. An example of this would be the challenge the Anglican church presently offers to John Paul II over the issue of women's ordination. John Paul has recently stated that Anglican inclusion of women as priests would detrimentally affect unity talks between the two churches. The Anglican communion is in a prophetic position to work toward justice for women, both internally and for the Christian church at large. Ruether's christology encourages Anglicans to do just that.

21. Ruether, "The Liberation of Christology from Patriarchy," 128.

22. See above, 81-88.

23. Ruether, *Disputed Questions*, 13.

24. Here I am using Paul Knitter's explanation of "kairos": "*Kairos*, especially as used by Paul Tillich, signifies those special moments in time that are different from ordinary time (*chronos*). It is a point in history when, because of the particular constellation of events and personalities, genuinely new possibilities and advance are latent. A *kairos* is not just a situation; it is also an opportunity. If we miss a *kairos*, we miss something very important. A burden of responsibility is tied into the recognition of a *kairos*." See Knitter, *No Other Name?*, 18.

25. Ruether, "Feminist Theology and Spirituality," 9.

26. Ibid., 18.

27. Knitter, *No Other Name?*, 204.

28. Ruether, "Feminist Theology and Spirituality," 22.

29. Ibid., 17.

30. Ibid., 22.

31 Ruether, *Womanguides*, 105. Regarding Ruether's use of the term God/ess she has written that it is "...a written symbol intended to combine both the masculine and feminine forms of the word for the divine while preserving the Judeo-Christian affirmation that divinity is one. This term is unpronounceable and inadequate. It is not intended as language for worship, where one might prefer a more evocative term, such as Holy One or Holy Wisdom. Rather it serves here as an analytic sign to point toward that yet unnameable understanding of the divine that would transcend patriarchal limitations and signal redemptive experience for women as well as men." See Ruether, *Sexism and God-Talk*, 46.

32. Ruether, *Sexism and God-Talk*, 161.

33. Ibid., 181.

34. Ruether, "Social Sin," 46.

35. Ruether, "Feminist Theology and Spirituality," 26.

36. Ruether, "Individual Repentance is Not Enough," *Explor* 2 (Spring 1976): 52.

## Epilogue

1. See Schüssler Fiorenza, *In Memory of Her*.

2. For criticisms of Ruether's presentation of history see Angela V. Askew, review of *Sexism and God-Talk: Toward a Feminist Theology*, by Rosemary Radford Ruether, *Union Seminary Quarterly Review*, 40 (1985): 66 and John M. Oesterreicher, "Anatomy of Contempt: A Critique of Rosemary Radford Ruether's 'Faith and Fratricide,'" *The Institute of Judaeo-Christian Studies* 4 (Fall 1975): 4-5.

3. Roger Haight, *An Alternative Vision: An Interpretation of Liberation Theology* (New York: Paulist Press, 1985), 122.

4. Heyward, "An Unfinished Symphony," 114.

# Bibliography

**By Rosemary Radford Ruether**
**In Chronological Order**

"Marriage, Love and Children." *Jubilee* 11 (December 1963): 17-20.

"A Question of Dignity, A Question of Freedom." In *What Modern Catholics Think About Birth Control*, edited by William Birmingham, 233-240. Toronto: The New American Library, 1964.

"Birth Control and the Ideals of Marital Sexuality." In *Contraception and Holiness*, edited by Thomas Roberts, S.J., 72-91. New York: Herder and Herder, 1964.

"Ministry in the Church of the Future." In *Secular Priest in the New Church*, edited by Gerard Sloyan, 232-249. New York: Herder and Herder, 1964.

"The Church Is a Happening." *Cross Currents* 15 (Spring 1965): 237-241.

"Is Roman Catholicism Reformable?" *The Christian Century* 82 (September 22, 1965): 1152-1154.

"Catholicism and Catholicity." *In The Generation of the Third Eye*, edited by Daniel Callahan, 186-194. New York: Sheed & Ward, 1965.

"Catholicism's Celibacy Crisis." *The Christian Century* 83 (October 19, 1966): 1268-1270.

"Post-Ecumenical Christianity." *The Ecumenist* 5 (November-December 1966): 3-7.

*The Church Against Itself: An Inquiry into the Conditions of Historical Existence for the Eschatological Community.* New York: Herder and Herder, 1967.

"Symposium on Women." *Commonweal* 85 (January 27, 1967): 446-458.

"The Becoming of Women in Church and Society." *Cross Currents* 17 (Fall 1967): 419-426.

"Theological Anti-Semitism in the New Testament." *The Christian Century* 85 (February 14, 1968): 191-196.

"Schism of Consciousness." *Commonweal* 88 (May 31, 1968): 326-331.

"Black Theology." *America* 120 (June 14, 1969): 684-687.

"The New Church." *Commonweal* 90 (April 4, 1969): 64-66.

"The Virginity of Mary and the Brothers of Jesus: The Collision of History and Doctrine." *Continuum* 7 (Winter/Spring 1969): 93-105.

"New Wine, Maybe New Wineskins for the Church." *The Christian Century* 86 (April 2, 1969): 445-449.

*Gregory of Nazianzus: Rhetor and Philosopher.* London: Oxford University Press, 1969.

"Preface." *Can These Bones Live?* Edited by Robert Lecky and Elliot Wright. New York: Sheed & Ward, 1969.

"The Ministry and the Eschatological Ethic." *Cross Currents* 19 (Spring 1969): 149-157.

"Beyond Confrontation: The Therapeutic Task." In *The Berrigans*, edited by William Van Etten Casey and Phillip Nobile, 113-121. New York: Avon, 1970.

"Education in the Sociological Situation, USA." In *Does the Church Know How to Teach?*, edited by Kendig Cully, 79-100. New York: Macmillan, 1970.

"Critic's Corner: An Unexpected Tribute to the Theologian." *Theology Today* 27 (October 1970): 332-339.

Review of *A Christocentric World History*, by Arend von Leeuwen. *Commonweal* 93 (December 4, 1970): 251-253.

"Radical Social Movement and the Radical Church Tradition." *Colloquium* 1, Oak Brook, Ilinois: Bethany Theological Seminary, 1970.

*The Radical Kingdom: The Western Experience of Messianic Hope.* New York: Paulist Press, 1970.

"A New Political Consciousness." *The Ecumenist* 8 (May-June 1970): 61-64.

"The Messianic Code." *Commonweal* 91 (January 16, 1970): 423-425.

"Male Chauvinist Theology and the Anger of Women." *Cross Currents* 21 (Spring 1971): 172-185.

"The Relevance of Martin Luther King for Today." In *Essays in Honor of Martin Luther King, Jr.*, edited by John H. Cartwright, 64-81. Evanston, Ilinois: Leiffer Bureau of Social and Religious Research, Garrett-Evangelical Theological Seminary, 1971.

"Christian Anti-Semitism—The Dilemma of Zionism." *Christianity and Crisis* 32 (April 17, 1972): 91-94.

*Liberation Theology: Human Hope Confronts Christian History and American Power*. New York: Paulist Press, 1972.

"Judaism and Christianity: Two Fourth-Century Religions." *Studies in Religion* 2 (Summer 1972): 1-10.

"In What Sense Can We Say That Jesus Was 'The Christ'?" *The Ecumenist* 10 (January-February 1972): 17-24.

"The Pharisees in First-Century Judaism." *The Ecumenist* 11 (November-December 1972): 1-6.

"Anti-Semitism and the State of Israel—Some Principles for Christians." *Christianity and Crisis* 34 (November 26, 1973): 240-244.

"Male Clericalism and the Dread of Women." *The Ecumenist* 11 (July-August 1973): 65-69.

"Sexism and the Theology of Liberation." *The Christian Century* 90 (December 12, 1973): 1224-1229.

"Paradoxes of Human Hope: The Messianic Horizon of Church and Society." *Theological Studies* 33 (1972): 235-252.

"The Believers' Church and Catholicity in the World Today." In *Confusion and Hope: Clergy, Laity and Church in Transition*, edited by Glenn Bucher, 113-124. Philadelphia: Fortress Press, 1974.

"Anti-Semitism in Christian Theology." *Theology Today* 30 (January 1974): 365-382.

"The Suffering Servant Myth." *Worldview* 17 (March 1974): 45-46.

"Augustine and Christian Political Theology." *Interpretation: A Journal of Bible and Theology*. 29 (July 1975): 252-265.

"Zionism and Racism." *Christianity and Crisis* 35 (December 22, 1975): 307-311.

"Beginnings: An Intellectual Autobiography." In *Journeys: The Impact of Personal Experience on Religious Thought*, edited by Gregory Baum, 34-56. New York: Paulist Press, 1975.

"Home and Work: Women's Roles and the Transformation of Values." *Theological Studies* 36 (December 1975): 647-659.

"Whatever Happened to Theology?" *Christianity and Crisis* 35 (May 12, 1975): 109-110.

"Women, Ecology and the Domination of Nature." *The Ecumenist* 14 (November-December 1975): 1-5.

*New Women/New Earth: Sexist Ideologies and Human Liberation.* New York: The Seabury Press, 1975.

"The Bible and Social Justice." *The Ecumenist* 14 (January-February 1976): 24-27.

"Libertarianism and Neo-Colonialism: The Two Faces of America." *Christianity and Crisis* 36 (August 16, 1976): 80-83.

"Letter to Sergio Torres and the Planners of the Conference." In *Theology in the Americas,* edited by Sergio Torres and John Eagleson, 84-86. Maryknoll, New York: Orbis Books, 1976.

"Individual Repentance Is Not Enough." *Explor* 2 (Spring 1976): 47-52.

"Women Priests and Church Tradition." In *Women Priests: A Catholic Commentary on the Vatican Declaration,* edited by Leonard Swidler and Arlene Swidler, 234-236. New York: Paulist Press, 1977.

"Toward New Solutions: Working Women and the Male Workday." *Christianity and Crisis* 37 (February 7, 1977): 3-8.

"The Ministry of the People and the Future Shape of the Church." In *Southeastern Studies* 1, edited by John I. Durham, 81-93. Wake Forest, North Carolina: Southeastern Baptist Theological Seminary, 1977.

*Mary: Feminine Face of the Church.* Philadelphia: Westminster Press, 1977.

"Prayer—Authentic Marriage of Contemplation and Social Witness." *New Catholic World* 220 (January-February 1977): 682-685.

"Time Makes Ancient Good Uncouth: The Catholic Report on Sexuality." *The Christian Century* 94 (August 3-10 1977): 682-685.

"The Books That Shape Lives." *The Christian Century* 94 (October 19, 1977): 962.

"The Biblical Vision of the Ecological Crisis." *The Christian Century* 95 (November 22, 1978): 1129-1132.

"You Shall Call No Man Father: Sexism, Hierarchy and Liberation." In *Women and the Word: Sermons,* edited by Helen Gray Crotwell, 92-99. Philadelphia: Fortress Press, 1978.

"God-Talk After the End of Christendom." *Commonweal* 105 (June 16, 1978): 369-375.

"The Sexuality of Jesus: What Do the Synoptics Say?" *Christianity and Crisis* 38 (May 29, 1978): 134-137.

"Rich Nations/Poor Nations: Towards a Just World Order in the Era of Neo-Colonialism." In *Christian Spirituality in the United States: Independence and Interdependence*, edited by Francis A. Eigo, O.S.A., 59-91. Villanova, Pennsylvania: Villanova University Press, 1978.

"Patristic Spirituality and the Experience of Women in the Early Church." In *Western Spirituality: The Historical Roots, Ecumenical Routes*, edited by Matthew Fox, 140-163. Notre Dame, Indiana: Fides/Claretian, 1979.

"The Adversus Judaeos Tradition in the Church Fathers: The Exegesis of Christian Anti-Judaism." In *Aspects of Jewish Culture in the Middle Ages*, edited by Paul E. Szmarch, 27-50. Albany: State University of New York Press, 1979.

*Faith and Fratricide: The Theological Roots of Anti-Semitism.* New York: Seabury Press, 1979.

"Consciousness Raising at Puebla: Women Speak to the Latin Church." *Christianity and Crisis* 39 (April 2, 1979): 77-80.

"Entering the Sanctuary: The Roman Catholic Story." In *Women of Spirit: Female Leadership in the Jewish and Christian Traditions*, edited by Rosemary Radford Ruether and Eleanor McLaughlin, 373-383. New York: Simon & Schuster, 1979.

"A Religion for Women: Sources and Strategies." *Christianity and Crisis* 39 (December 10, 1979): 307-311.

"Motherearth and the Megamachine." In *Womanspirit Rising: A Feminist Reader in Religion*, edited by Carol P. Christ and Judith Plaskow, 43-52. San Francisco: Harper & Row, 1979.

"Mothers of the Church: Ascetic Women in the Late Patristic Age." In *Women of Spirit: Female Leadership in the Jewish and Christian Traditions*, edited by Rosemary Radford Ruether and Eleanor McLaughlin, 72-98. New York: Simon & Schuster, 1979.

"Ruether on Ruether." *Christianity and Crisis* 39 (May 14, 1979): 126.

"Politics and the Family." *Christianity and Crisis* 40 (September 29, 1980): 261-266.

"Asking the Existential Questions." *The Christian Century* 97 (April 2, 1980): 374-378.

"Why Socialism Needs Feminism and Vice Versa." *Christianity and Crisis* 40 (April 28, 1980): 103-108.

"Goddesses and Witches: Liberation and Countercultural Feminism." *The Christian Century* 97 (September 10-17, 1980): 842-847.

"Why Males Fear Women Priests: Historical Analysis." *Witness* 63 (July 1980): 19-21.

"Women in Utopian Movements." In *Women and Religion in America: The 19th Century, Volume I*, edited by Rosemary Radford Ruether and Rosemary Skinner Keller, 46-100. San Francisco: Harper & Row, 1981.

"The Feminist Critique in Religious Studies." *Soundings* 64 (Winter 1981): 388-402.

"Basic Christian Communities: Introduction." *Christianity and Crisis* 41 (September 21, 1981): 234-237.

*To Change the World: Christology and Cultural Criticism.* New York: Crossroad, 1981.

"Social Sin." *Commonweal* 108 (January 30, 1981): 46-48.

"The Female Nature of God: A Problem in Contemporary Religious Life." *Concilium 143 Religion in the Eighties: God as Father?* Edited by Johannes Baptist Metz and Edward Schillebeeckx. Edinburgh: T.& T. Clark, Ltd. and New York: Seabury Press, 1981, 61-66.

"Christology and Jewish-Christian Relations." In *Jews and Christians after the Holocaust*, edited by Abraham Peck, 25-38. Philadelphia: Fortress Press, 1982.

"Introduction." *Threatened with Resurrection: Prayers and Poems from an Exiled Guatemalan*, by Julia Esquivel. Elgin, Ilinois: Brethren Press, 1982.

"Feminism and Patriarchal Religion: Principles of Ideological Critique of the Bible." *Journal for the Study of the Old Testament* 22 (1982): 54-66.

*Disputed Question: On Being a Christian.* Nashville: Abingdon, 1982.

Review of *Christ in a Changing World: Toward an Ethical Christology*, by Tom Driver. *The Christian Century* 99 (April 7, 1982): 416-420.

"Woman as Oppressed; Woman as Liberated in the Scriptures." In *Spinning a Sacred Yarn: Women Speak from the Pulpit*, 181-186. New York: Pilgrim Press, 1982.

"Courage as a Christian Virtue." *Cross Currents* 33 (Spring 1983): 8-16.

"The Family, in a Dim Light." *Christianity and Crisis* 43 (June 27, 1983): 263-266.

"Triple Oppression: Sex, Class and Race." In *God and Human Freedom: Festschrift in Honor of Howard Thurman*, edited by Henry T. Young, 33-43. Richmond, Indiana: Friends United Press, 1983.

*Sexism and God-Talk: Toward a Feminist Theology*. Boston: Beacon Press, 1983.

Review of *Christ, the Experience of Jesus as Lord*, by Edward Schillebeeckx. *Religious Studies Review* 9 (January 1983): 42-44.

"Feminism and Peace." *The Christian Century* 100 (August 31-September 7, 1983): 771-776.

"An Unrealized Revolution: Searching the Scriptures for a Model of the Family." *Christianity and Crisis* 43 (October 31, 1983): 399-404.

"Theology from the Side of the Other." *Soundings* 5 (November 1983): 6-7.

"Women in Ministry: Where Are They Heading?" *Christianity and Crisis* 43 (April 4, 1983): 111-116.

"Feminist Theology and Spirituality." In *Christian Feminism: Vision of a New Humanity*, edited by Judith Weidman, 9-32. San Francisco: Harper & Row, 1984.

"Envisioning Our Hopes: Some Models of the Future." In *Women's Spirit Bonding*, edited by Mary I. Buckley and Janet Kalven, 325-335. New York: Pilgrim Press, 1984.

"Review Symposium: *In Memory of Her: A Feminist Theological Reconstruction of Christian Origins*, by Elisabeth Schussler Fiorenza." *Horizons* 11 (Spring 1984): 146-150.

"Feminist Theology in the Academy." *Christianity and Crisis* 45 (March 4, 1985): 57-62.

"Feminist Interpretation: A Method of Correlation." In *Feminist Interpretation of the Bible*, edited by Letty M. Russell, 111-112. Philadelphia: The Westminster Press, 1985.

*Womanguides: Readings Toward a Feminist Theology*. Boston: Beacon Press, 1985.

"Sex: Female; Religion: Catholic; Forecast: Fair." *U.S. Catholic* 50 (April 1985): 19-26.

"Catholics and Abortion: Authority and Dissent." *The Christian Century* 102 (October 2, 1985): 859-862.

"A Feminist Perspective." In *Doing Theology in a Divided World*, edited by Virginia Fabella and Sergio Torres, 65-71. Maryknoll, New York: Orbis Books, 1985.

"The Future of Feminist Theology in the Academy." *Journal of the American Academy of Religion* 53 (December 1985): 703-713.

"The Liberation of Christology from Patriarchy." *Religion and Intellectual Life* 2 (Spring 1985): 116-128.

*Women-Church: Theology and Practice of Feminist Liturgical Communities*. San Francisco: Harper & Row, 1985.

"Feminism and Religious Faith: Renewal or New Creation?" *Religion and Intellectual Life* 3 (Winter 1986): 7-20.

"Crises and Challenges of Catholicism Today." *America* 154 (March 1, 1986): 152-164.

*Contemporary Roman Catholicism: Crises and Challenges*. Kansas City, Missouri: Sheed & Ward, 1987.

"Feminism and Jewish-Christian Dialogue." In *The Myth of Christian Uniqueness: Toward a Pluralistic Theology of Religions*, edited by John Hick and Paul F. Knitter, 137-148. Maryknoll, New York: Orbis Books, 1987.

Ed. *Religion and Sexism: Images of Women in the Jewish and Christian Traditions*. New York: Simon & Schuster, 1974.

_____and Herman Ruether. "Zionism and Racism." *Christianity and Crisis* 35 (December 22, 1975): 307-311.

_____and Eugene C. Bianchi. *From Machismo to Mutuality: Essays on Sexism and Woman-Man Liberation*. New York: Paulist Press, 1976.

_____and Eleanor McLaughlin. "Woman's Leadership in the Jewish and Christian Traditions: Continuity and Change." In *Women of Spirit: Female Leadership in the Jewish and Christian Traditions*, edited by Rosemary Radford Ruether and Eleanor McLaughlin, 15-28. New York: Simon & Schuster, 1979.

_____and Rosemary Skinner Keller, eds. *Women and Religion in America: The 19th Century, Volume I*. San Francisco: Harper & Row, 1981.

## Special Sources

"Messiah of Israel and the Cosmic Christ: A Study of the Development of Christology in Judaism and Early Christianity." Unpublished manuscript. Washington, D.C., 1971.

Letter to Author, 25 November 1984.

Letter to Author, 26 March 1985.

Letter to Author, 10 March 1986.


## Other Works Consulted

Anderson, Gerald H. and Thomas F. Stransky. *Christ's Lordship and Religious Pluralism*. Maryknoll, New York: Orbis Books, 1983.

Andolsen, Barbara Hilkert, Christine E. Gudorf and Mary D. Pellauer. Women's Consciousness, *Women's Conscience: A Reader in Feminist Ethics*. Minneapolis: Winston Press, 1985.

Askew, Angela V. Review of *Sexism and God-Talk: Toward a Feminist Theology*, by Rosemary Radford Ruether. *Union Seminary Quarterly Review* 40 (1985): 59-68.

Aulen, G. *Christus Victor: An Historical Study of the Three Main Types of the Idea of the Atonement*. New York: Macmillan, 1969.

Baum, Gregory. *Is the New Testament Anti-Semitic?* New York: Paulist Press, 1965.

_____. "Introduction." *Faith and Fratricide: The Theological Roots of Anti-Semitism*, by Rosemary Radford Ruether. New York: Seabury Press, 1979, 1-22.

_____, ed. *Sociology and Human Destiny*. New York: Seabury Press, 1980.

Bettenhausen, Elizabeth, *et. al.* "A Feminist Future: Responses and Reflections." *Christianity and Crisis* 45 (April 29, 1985): 158-165.

Bonino, José Míguez, ed. *Faces of Jesus: Latin American Christologies*. Maryknoll, New York: Orbis Books, 1984.

Bussman, Claus. *Who Do You Say? Jesus Christ in Latin American Theology*. Translated by Robert Barr. Maryknoll, New York: Orbis Books, 1985.

Cardman, Francine. "The Emperor's New Clothes: Christ and Constantine." In *Above Every Name: The Lordship of Christ and Social Systems*, edited by Thomas E. Clarke, 191-210. New York: Paulist Press, 1980.

_____. Review of *To Change the World: Christology and Cultural Criticism*, by Rosemary Radford Ruether. *Spirituality Today* 34 (Summer 1982): 180-181.

Cardoso, Fernando Henrique and Enzo Faletto. Dependency and *Development in Latin America*. Translated by Marjory Mattingly Urquidi. Berkeley: University of California Press, 1979.

Christ, Carol P. *Laughter of Aphrodite: Reflections on a Journey to the Goddess*. San Francisco: Harper & Row, 1987.

_____ and Judith Plaskow, eds. *Womanspirit Rising: A Feminist Reader in Religion*. San Francisco: Harper & Row, 1979.

Cormie, Lee. "The Sociology of National Development and Salvation History." In *Sociology and Human Destiny*, edited by Gregory Baum, 56-85. New York: Seabury Press, 1980.

D'Angelo, Mary Rose. "Remembering Her: Feminist Readings of the Christian Tradition." *Toronto Journal of Theology* 2 (1981): 118-126.

Davies, Alan, ed. *Anti-Semitism and the Foundations of Christianity*. New York: Paulist Press, 1979.

Dillistone, Frederick W. *The Christian Understanding of Atonement*. Philadelphia: Westminster Press, 1968.

Driver, Tom F. *Christ in a Changing World: Toward an Ethical Christology*. New York: Crossroad, 1981.

Ferm, Deane William. *Contemporary American Theologies: A Critical Survey*. New York: Seabury Press, 1981.

Friedan, Betty, *The Feminine Mystique*. New York: Dell Publishing Company, 1963.

Fuller, Reginald and Pheme Perkins. *Who is this Christ?: Gospel Christology and Contemporary Faith*. Philadelphia: Fortress Press, 1983.

Grillmeir, Aloys, S.J. *Christ in the Christian Tradition, I* Translated by John Bowden. Atlanta: John Knox Press, 1975.

Gutiérrez, Gustavo. *A Theology of Liberation*. Maryknoll, New York: Orbis Books, 1973.

Haight, Roger. *An Alternative Vision: An Interpretation of Liberation Theology*. New York: Paulist Press, 1985.

Hayter, Theresa. *The Creation of World Poverty*. London: Pluto Press, 1983.

Hellwig, Monika. "Christology." In *An American Catholic Catechism*, edited by George Dyer, 66-77. New York: Seabury Press, 1975.

_____. "Bases and Boundaries for Interfaith Dialogue: A Christian Viewpoint." *Journal of Ecumenical Studies* 14 (1977): 419-431.

_____. "Liberation Theology: An Emerging School." *Scottish Journal of Theology* 30 (1977): 137-151.

_____. "From the Jesus of Story to the Christ of Dogma." In *Anti-Semitism and the Foundations of Christianity*, edited by Alan T. Davies, 118-136. New York: Paulist Press, 1979.

_____. "Christology and Attitudes Toward Social Structures." In *Above Every Name: The Lordship of Christ and Social Systems*, edited by Thomas E. Clarke, 13-34. New York: Paulist Press, 1980.

_____. "Changing Soteriology in Ecumenical Context: A Catholic Reflection." *Proceedings of the Catholic Theological Society of America*. 38 (June 1983): 14-21.

_____. *Jesus the Compassion of God*. Wilmington, Delaware: Michael Glazier, Inc., 1983.

Heyward, Carter. "Speaking and Sparking, Building and Burning." *Christianity and Crisis* 39 (April 2, 1979): 66-72.

_____. *The Redemption of God: A Theology of Mutual Relation*. Washington, D.C.: University Press of America, 1982.

_____. "An Unfinished Symphony of Liberation: The Radicalization of Christian Feminism Among White U.S. Women: A Review Essay." *Journal of Feminist Studies in Religion* I (Spring 1985): 99-118.

Hick, John and Paul F. Knitter, eds. *The Myth of Christian Uniqueness: Toward a Pluralistic Theology of Religions*. Maryknoll, New York: Orbis Books, 1987.

Holtz, Barry W. "Midrash." In *Back to the Sources: Reading the Classic Jewish Texts*, edited by Barry Holtz, 177-212. New York: Summit Books, 1984.

Johnson, Elizabeth A., C.S.J. "The Incomprehensibility of God and the Image of God Male and Female." *Theological Studies* 45 (1984): 441-465.

_____. "Seminar on Christology." *Proceedings of the Catholic Theological Society of America* 39 (1984): 153-155.

_____. "Jesus, The Wisdom of God: A Biblical Basis for Non-Androcentric Christology." *Emphemerides Theologicae Lovanienses* 61 (December 1985): 261-294.

_____. "Seminar on Christology." *Proceedings of the Catholic Theological Society of America* 40 (1985): 184-187.

Kelly, J.N.D. *Early Christian Doctrines.* New York: Harper & Row, 1960.

Knitter, Paul. "European Protestant and Catholic Approaches to the World Religions: Complements and Contrasts." *Journal of Ecumenical Studies* 12 (1975): 13-29.

_____. "World Religions and the Finality of Christ: A Critique of Hans Küng's *On Being a Christian.*" Horizons 5 (Fall 1978): 151-164.

_____. "Jesus-Buddha-Krishna: Still Present?" *Journal of Ecumenical Studies* 16 (Fall 1979): 651-671.

_____. "Christianity as Religion: True and Absolute? A Roman Catholic Perspective." *Concilium* 136 *What is Religion: An Inquiry for Christian Theology?* Edited by David Tracy and Mircea Eliade. New York: Seabury Press, 1980, pp. 12-21.

_____. "Theocentric Christology." *Theology Today* 40 (July 1983): 130-149.

_____. *No Other Name? A Critical Survey of Christian Attitudes Toward the Religions.* Maryknoll, New York: Orbis Press, 1985.

_____. "Toward a Liberation Theology of Religions." In *The Myth of Christian Uniqueness: Toward a Pluralistic Theology of Religions,* edited by John Hick and Paul F. Knitter, 178-200. Maryknoll, New York: Orbis Books, 1987.

Kuhn, Thomas. *The Structure of Scientific Revolutions.* Second Edition. Chicago: University of Chicago Press, 1970.

Lakeland, Paul. *Freedom in Christ: An Introduction to Political Theology.* New York: Fordham University Press, 1986.

Lamb, Matthew L. *Solidarity with Victims: Toward a Theology of Social Transformation.* New York: Crossroad, 1982.

Leonard, Ellen. Review of *Sexism and God-Talk: Toward a Feminist Theology,* by Rosemary Radford Ruether. *The Ecumenist* 23 (May-June 1985): 61-63.

_____. "The Contribution of Feminism to Theological Studies." Unpublished paper. Toronto, Ontario, 1986.

McDermott, Brian O., S.J. "Roman Catholic Christology: Two Recurring Themes." *Theological Studies* 41 (1980): 339-367.

McGarry, Michael B. *Christology after Auschwitz*. New York: Paulist Press, 1977.

Micks, Marianne. Review of *To Change the World: Christology and Cultural Criticism*, by Rosemary Radford Ruether. *Theology Today* 39 (July 1982): 214-215.

Mullins, Mary. Review of *New Woman, New Earth: Sexist Ideologies and Human Liberation*, by Rosemary Radford Ruether. *Horizons* 6 (Spring 1979): 129-130.

Mowinckel, Sigmund. *He That Cometh*. New York: Blackwell and Abingdon, 1955.

Nolan, Albert. *Jesus Before Christianity*. Maryknoll, New York: Orbis Books, 1976.

Norris, Richard A. *The Christological Controversy*. Philadelphia: Fortress Press, 1980.

O'Collins, Gerald. *What Are They Saying About Jesus?* New York: Paulist Press, 1977.

Oesterreicher, John M. *Anatomy of Contempt: A Critique of Rosemary Radford Ruether's "Faith and Fratricide."* *The Institute of Judaeo-Christian Studies* 4 (Fall 1975): 1-45.

Ogden, Schubert M. *The Point of Christology*. San Francisco: Harper & Row, 1982.

Osiek, Carolyn. *Beyond Anger: On Being a Feminist in the Church*. New York: Paulist Press, 1986.

Pagels, Elaine. "Women, the Bible and Human Nature." Review of *Womanguides: Readings Toward a Feminist Theology*, by Rosemary Radford Ruether and *Bread Not Stone: The Challenge of Feminist Biblical Interpretation*, by Elisabeth Schüssler Fiorenza. *The New York Times Book Review* (April 1, 1985): 3, 19.

Pawlikowski, John T., O.S.M. *Christ in the Light of the Christian-Jewish Dialogue*. New York: Paulist Press, 1982.

Pellauer, Mary. Review of *Sexism and God-Talk: Toward a Feminist Theology*, by Rosemary Radford Ruether. *Theology Today* 40 (April 1983): 472-474.

Pieris, Aloysius. "Speaking of the Son of God in Non-Christian Cultures, e.g., in Asia." *Concilium* 153 *Jesus, Son of God?* Edited by Edward Schillebeeckx and Johannes-Baptist Metz. New York: Seabury Press, 1982, 73-77.

Pixley, George. *God's Kingdom: A Guide for Biblical Study.* Translated by Donald D. Walsh. Maryknoll, New York: Orbis Books, 1981.

Rahner, Karl. *Foundations of Christian Faith: An Introduction to the Idea of Christianity.* Translated by William V. Dych. New York: Seabury Press, 1978, 178-310.

_____. "Christology Today." *Concilium* 153 *Jesus, Son of God?* Edited by Edward Schillebeeckx and Johannes-Baptist Metz. New York: Seabury Press, 1982, 73-77.

_____. "Soteriology." *Sacramentum Mundi* 3 Edited by Karl Rahner, with Cornelius Ernst and Kevin Smyth. London: Burns & Oates Ltd., 1970, 435-438.

Ramsay, William. *Four Modern Prophets: Walter Raushenbush, Gustavo Gitierrez, Martin Luther King, Jr., Rosemary Radford Ruether.* Atlanta: John Knox Press, 1986.

Richard, Lucien. *What Are They Saying About Christ and World Religions?* New York: Paulist Press, 1981.

Rogers, Jack, Ross Mackenzie and Louis Weeks. *Case Studies in Christ and Salvation.* Philadelphia: The Westminister Press, 1977.

Schillebeeckx, Edward. *Jesus: An Experiment in Christology.* New York: Seabury Press, 1979.

Schineller, Peter J., S.J. "Christ and the Church: A Spectrum of Views." *Theological Studies* 37 (1976): 545-566.

Schneiders, Sandra M. *Women and the Word: The Sender of God in the New Testament and the Spirituality of Women.* New York: Paulist Press, 1986.

Schüssler Fiorenza, Elisabeth. "Wisdom Mythology and the Christological Hymns of the New Testament." In *Aspects of Wisdom in Judaism and Early Christianity*, edited by Robert Wilken, 17-41. Notre Dame, Indiana: University of Notre Dame Press, 1975.

_____. *In Memory of Her: A Feminist Theological Reconstruction of Christian Origins.* New York: Crossroad, 1983.

_____. "For Women in Men's Worlds: A Critical Feminist Theology of Liberation." *Concilium* 171 *Different Theologies, Common Responsibility: Babel or Pentecost?* Edited by Claude Geffre, Gustavo Gutiérrez and Virgilio Elizondo. Edingburgh: T. & T. Clarke, Ltd., 1984, 32-39.

_____. "Breaking Silence—Becoming Visible." *Concilium* 185 *Women—Invisible in Church and Society.* Edited by Elisabeth Schüssler-Fiorenza and Mary Collins. Edingburgh: T. & T. Clarke, Ltd., 1985, 3-16.

_____, et al. "On Feminist Methodology." *Journal of Feminist Studies in Religion* I (Fall 1985): 73-88.

Schüssler Fiorenza, Francis. "Critical Social Theory and Christology: Toward an Understanding of Atonement and Redemption as Emancipatory Solidarity." *Proceedings of the Catholic Theological Society of America* 30 (1975) 63-110.

_____. "Christology After Vatican II." *The Ecumenist* 18 (September-October 1980): 81-89.

Segundo, Juan Luis. "Capitalism Versus Socialism: Crux Theologica." In *Frontiers of Theology in Latin America*, edited by Rosino Gibellini, 240-259. Maryknoll, New York: Orbis Books, 1978.

Shields, David L. *Growing Beyond Prejudices: Overcoming Hierarchical Dualism*. Mystic, Connecticut: Twenty-Third Publications, 1986.

Sobrino, Jon. *Christology at the Crossroads*. Maryknoll, New York: Orbis Books, 1978.

_____. "A Crucified People's Faith in the Son of God." *Concilium* 153 *Jesus, Son of God?* Edited by Edward Schillebeeckx and Johannes-Baptist Metz. New York: Seabury Press, 1982, 23-28.

Tennis, Diane. Review of *Women-Church: Theology and Practice of Feminist Liturgical Communities*, by Rosemary Radford Ruether. *Theology Today* 54 (April 1987): 139-142.

Thompson, William M. *The Jesus Debate: A Survey and Synthesis*. New York: Paulist Press, 1985.

_____. "Dappled and Deep Down Things: A Meditation on Christian Ecological Trends." *Horizons* 14 (Spring 1987): 64-81.

Vaughan, Judith. *Sociality, Ethics and Social Change: A Critical Appraisal of Reinhold Niebuhr's Ethics in the Light of Rosemary Radford Ruether's Works*. Lanham, Maryland: University of America Press, 1983.

Van Bavel, Tarcisius. "Chalcedon: Then and Now." *Concilium* 153 *Jesus, Son of God?* Edited by Edward Schillebeeckx and Johannes-Baptist Metz. New York: The Seabury Press, 1982, 23-28.

Weaver, Mary Jo. *New Catholic Women: A Contemporary Challenge to Traditional Religious Authority*. San Francisco: Harper & Row, 1985.

Weir, Mary Kathryn Williams. "The Concept of Freedom in the Work of Rosemary Radford Ruether." Ph.D. diss., the University of St. Andrew's, Scotland, 1982.

Wilson-Kastner, Patricia. *Faith, Feminism and the Christ*. Philadelphia: Fortress Press, 1983.

# Index